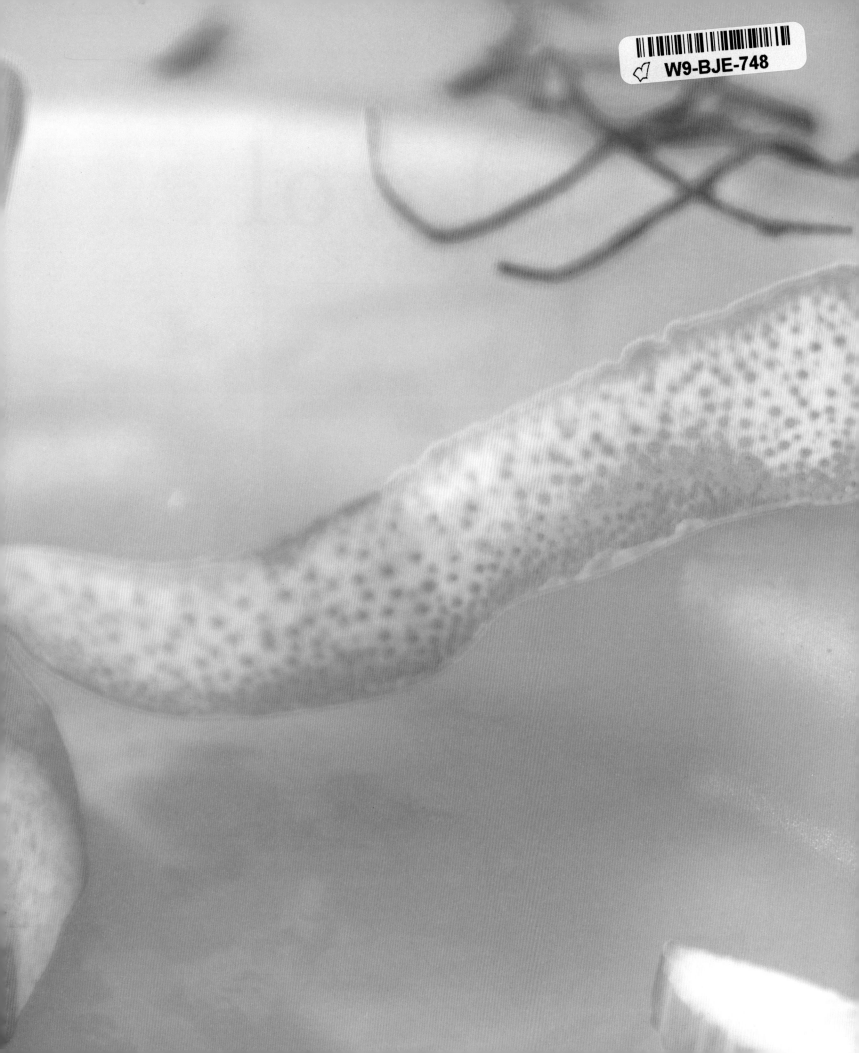

complete

low fat

cooking

First published in Great Britain in 1998 by
Hamlyn, a division of Octopus Publishing Group Limited
2–4 Heron Quays, London E14 4JP

Reprinted 2001

ISBN 0 600 60524 8

M 10 9 8 7 6 5 4 3 2 1

NOTES
Eggs should be medium to large unless otherwise stated.
The USDA advises that eggs should not be consumed raw. This
book contains dishes made with raw or lightly cooked eggs. It is
prudent for more vulnerable people such as pregnant and nursing
mothers, invalids, the elderly, babies, and young children to avoid
uncooked or lightly cooked dishes made with eggs. Once
prepared, these dishes should be kept refrigerated and used
promptly.

Meat and poultry should be cooked thoroughly. To test if poultry
is cooked, pierce the flesh through the thickest part with a skewer
or fork — the juices should run clear, never pink or red. Do not
re-freeze poultry that has been frozen previously and thawed. Do
not re-freeze a cooked dish that has been frozen previously.
Milk should be whole milk unless otherwise stated.

Nut and Nut Derivatives
This book includes dishes made with nuts and nut derivatives. It
is advisable for those with known allergic reactions to nuts and
nut derivatives and those who may be potentially vulnerable to
these allergies, such as pregnant and nursing mothers, invalids,
the elderly, babies, and children to avoid dishes made with nuts
and nut oils. It is also prudent to check the labels of pre-prepared
ingredients for the possible inclusion of nut derivatives.

Pepper should be freshly ground black pepper unless otherwise
stated.

Fresh herbs should be used, unless otherwise stated. If
unavailable, use dried herbs as an alternative, but halve the
quantities stated.

Ovens should be pre-heated to the specified temperature — if
using a fan-assisted oven, follow the manufacturer's instructions
for adjusting the cooking time and the temperature.

Vegetarians should ensure that cheese is made with vegetarian
rennet. There are vegetarian forms of Parmesan, feta, Cheddar,
Monterey Jack, Cheshire, Red Leicester, dolcelatte, and many
goats' cheeses.

All recipes have been analyzed per serving by a professional
nutritionist.

Contents

Introduction

The determination to follow a healthy diet now appears routinely on practically everyone's list of New Year's resolutions, whether the aim is one of general good health or simply to lose weight. Everyone wants to feel fit and well, and most people would also like to shed a few pounds.

One of the easiest ways of achieving both these admirable aims at one fell swoop is to follow a low-fat diet. This is what this book aims to convince you to do and — still more important — shows you how to do it.

Most of us consume more fat today than ever before. The addition of fat gives food a pleasantly rich flavor, as well as a creamy texture that helps it slide satisfyingly down the throat with alarming ease!

But we shouldn't burden ourselves with guilt about our addiction to fat. Apparently we can't help it. Research conducted by Rockefeller University has shown that the more fat we eat, the more we actually crave, thereby setting up a vicious cycle that it is very hard to escape.

Why reduce fat?

The arguments for reducing the fat in the diet are compelling. Put quite simply, fat is not only fattening, it is also bad for us.

It is believed by some doctors that too high an intake of fat may promote some forms of cancer, particularly colon, prostate, and breast cancers. It has also been suggested that eating less fat may reduce the incidence of atherosclerosis (deposits of excess fat on the artery walls), thereby decreasing the risk of heart attacks and strokes.

Last but by no means least, particularly for anyone who has trouble maintaining their weight, a low-fat diet will also make it easier to keep slim, especially if you also take regular exercise. Your general health and sense of well-being should improve dramatically if you follow a low-fat diet, and your general resistance to infection will also improve.

Some fat is necessary

Reducing fat does not, however, mean eliminating it completely— even if that were possible. A certain amount of fat is necessary for a balanced diet. It is essential to health.

Essential fats, as they are called, are believed to be essential for certain human functions. These include brain function, maintenance of the immune and nervous systems, and regulation of the hormonal balance.

Some forms of fat are much worse than others. Saturated fats, for example, which are solid at room temperature and usually derive from animal sources, such as the fat in meat and poultry, butter, lard, and cheese, are particularly bad. They tend to encourage the liver to produce more cholesterol, and to make the blood more prone to clotting.

Restrict your intake of fats as much as possible to unsaturated fats— those which are liquid at room temperature — such as most vegetable oils (with the exception of coconut oil and palm oil, both of which are

just as delicious as its fattier — and, as a result, unhealthy counterparts.

Complete Low Fat is, rather, a collection of carefully planned recipes which make it possible to monitor the fats consumed without compromising on taste. The recipes in this book have all been carefully devised and nutritionally analyzed so that any cook can find the inspiration to make delicious meals, which will also contribute to a healthier, leaner, way of eating.

You will no doubt be surprised — not to say relieved — to see that there are some old favorites on these pages, proving that you don't have to give up any of these. You'll find, for example, classic dishes, such as Traditional Roast Turkey, Italian Veal Casserole, Tagliatelle alla Siciliana, and Strawberry Ice Cream, all of which have been made with a dramatically reduced fat content, which has in no way compromised the delicious flavor of the ingredients.

In addition, you will also be glad to find a great many interesting and exciting new recipes to add to your repertoire. Try Smoked Chicken with Peach Purée, Chicken with Fresh Mango Sauce, Stuffed Grape Leaves with Chicken Livers, Haddock and Cider Casserole, Venison Marinated in Beer, Pumpkin Curry, Spanish Coleslaw, Couscous with Hot Peppers, Pears with Fresh Raspberry Sauce, and Sliced Figs with Lemon Sauce. So you thought that low fat eating was boring? No siree! We can guarantee that you will get absolutely no complaints at all from your tastebuds!

saturated fats). Monounsaturated fats, such as olive oil, are preferable to polyunsaturated fats, such as safflower and sunflower oils, as they do not raise the blood cholesterol levels.

One particular form of polyunsaturated fat, however, which is found in fish oils — particularly in oily fish such as salmon, mackerel, tuna, herring, and trout — is especially healthful as it is thought to help prevent thrombosis and to reduce the risk of heart disease.

To sum up, most fats are bad for us and should be eaten in very small amounts, if at all. A few, however, are good and some fat is essential for good health. Overall, though, the best policy is to reduce the general level of all fat in your diet, and this is what *Complete Low Fat* aims to show you how to do.

No sacrifice

This book is not about giving up all the delicious things that we like to eat. Nor is it a fad diet book. Low-fat food does not mean making any kind of sacrifice — it can be

"We are not suggesting that you should never eat any of your old favorites ... ever again."

The end of steaks, hamburgers, French fries, and hold the mayo?

We are not suggesting that you should never again eat any of your old favorites, such as steaks, hamburgers, sloppy joes, French fries, and salads smothered in mayonnaise. Our traditional idea of wholesome, delicious foods is rooted in dishes such as these, and there is absolutely nothing wrong with them — as long as they are consumed IN MODERATION.

But one must bear in mind that the incidence of coronary heart disease has increased dramatically in the past 50 years or so, and that medical research has identified several major causes. One of these is too high a consumption of saturated fats and too high a level of cholesterol in the diet. The foods that many of us eat in the greatest quantities — day in, day out — such as red meats and dairy foods, are the biggest culprits of all. These are the foods that we need to eat less of. But that is not as depressing as it sounds. There are, of course, a great many other delicious foods to eat, and this book aims to nudge you, persuasively but gently, in the right direction.

So what should we eat?

The question of fat in our diets is a complex one. No one single food contains just one type of fat.

It is rather the relative proportion of the different types of fat within any particular food that makes it healthy or unhealthy and that dictates whether or not it should be included in the diet.

What follows is a brief guide to the main food groups — dairy products, meat, fish, fruits, and vegetables, and so on — and their value in our diet.

Dairy Produce

One of the main sources of saturated fats in our diet comes in the form of dairy produce, such as milk, butter, cream, cheese, and ice cream. Sometimes all you need do is to choose low-fat versions of the usual dairy foods that you buy routinely.

Try, for example, to replace whole milk with semi-skim or, better still, skim milk. Cream substitutes, based on polyunsaturated fats, and low-fat ice-creams, can all contribute to lowering the intake of saturated fats. Plain low-fat yogurt and low-fat hard cheese, cottage cheese, and pot cheese can also help reduce the level of fat in your diet considerably.

Meats

Watching your fat intake does not mean giving up all meat. But you must be careful about how much of it, and which kind, you eat. Try to limit your portions of meat to about 3 ounces (about 3 average slices) and choose the leanest cuts possible whenever you can.

Remove all traces of visible fat before cooking the meat. It is better to grind very lean cuts of steak, such as sirloin, yourself, or ask the butcher to do it for you, rather than buy prepackaged ground meat, which gives you absolutely no control over the proportion of fat and lean.

When you roast meat, always place a rack in the bottom of the roasting pan so that the meat does not actually sit in its own juices. Try to roast it for a longer period of time but at a lower temperature — say, 350°F — so that the meat is not seared, as this would have the effect of sealing in the fat.

Broiling and barbecuing are considerably healthier methods of cooking than frying, as they do not need to involve any additional fat. When you broil meat, try adding extra flavor by marinating it first in herbs, wine,

Chicken and turkey are a lot leaner, for example, than goose and duck, though the fat in these meats is, at least, rather less saturated than that in red meats. Most of the fat in poultry is found just beneath the skin, so it is advisable always to remove the skin and to trim away all visible fat before cooking.

The best cooking methods are poaching, sautéing, broiling, stir-frying, and barbecuing. These are all healthy cooking methods, precisely because they need very little oil. Keep the temperature high and keep the food moving constantly in the wok or pan.

Microwaving is another good way of cooking without adding extra fat. Indeed, you can actually drain food of extra fat by placing it between two sheets of absorbent paper towels while it is cooking.

Fish and Shellfish

Fish is often recommended by nutritionists, dieticians, and doctors as one of the healthiest foods available. It is an excellent source of protein, while at the same time containing hardly any fat at all. Fish with a particularly low fat content include cod, red snapper, haddock, hake, and skate. Fish is also generally low in cholesterol. It is therefore an extremely good alternative to meat.

Fatty fish, such as mackerel, herring, sardines, tuna, salmon, and trout, are all excellent sources of polyunsaturated oils, which are believed to have a particularly protective effect on the circulation by making the blood platelets less sticky and consequently less liable to clot. This explains why the Inuit, whose diet consists of such large quantities of fish, have such a low incidence of heart disease.

According to many nutritionists and doctors, it is a good idea to eat fish at least two or three times a week, and to eat fatty fish at least once a week. If you like to eat canned fish, such as sardines, salmon, or tuna, read the labels carefully when you buy them and choose those that have been preserved in a named, healthy oil, such as soya, sunflower, or olive, rather than in an unspecified "vegetable" oil which is probably of inferior quality.

Steaming, poaching, and microwaving are all good methods of cooking fresh fish. Cooking whole fish in packages of aluminum foil or parchment paper with

garlic, and tomato or lemon juice. Barbecuing and grilling, where the heat comes from below the food instead of from above, as in broiling, is another good method, as long as the meat is basted with very little fat.

If you casserole or stew meat, it is always a good idea, if at all possible, to cook it on the day before you actually want to eat it. Chill the stew after cooking it, then skim off any solidified fat before you complete the cooking time, or reheat it just before eating.

Sausage links and processed meats often contain a high proportion of hidden fats — you can't actually see them but they're there! — which have been added as part of the preparation. To avoid these as much as possible, always read the labels carefully before buying and try to select those that have no more than 10% fat by weight.

Poultry and game

Poultry, or white meats, and game, such as quail, venison, buffalo, rabbit, and pheasant, are nearly always a lot lower in fat than red meats and contain a lot more polyunsaturated fat and less saturated fat than other meats. Be careful, though, to choose lean varieties.

seasonings, herbs, and flavorings is a highly recommended way of preparing it as it seals in all the flavor without there being a need to add any extra fat during the cooking process.

Many other types of seafood, such as shrimp, lobster, clams, and crab, are low in fat, although weight for weight some types of shellfish, such as shrimp, actually contain a higher level of cholesterol than meat and poultry. However, even these can be eaten occasionally without causing any risk to health.

Fruits, Vegetables, Grains, and Legumes
These foods contain absolutely no cholesterol and tend to be low in fat and high in fiber and vitamins. It is true that olives and avocados are exceptions and are both high in fat but, as the fat is largely unsaturated, their intake needs to be limited only for their high calorie count.

Be careful to check the labels on processed foods made from vegetables, grains, or legumes for fats that have been added during processing. Breads and pastas made with egg yolk should be avoided because the egg also increases their fat content. You should also check that processed vegetables have not had salt or sodium added during their preparation. As a general rule, fresh produce is always better than packaged, canned, or frozen foods.

Vegetables and salads come in an enormous variety and can be prepared in a great many different ways. Steamed vegetables contain no fat at all and a fresh green salad can be heaped on the plate in virtually unlimited quantities, as long as no oil is added to the dressing for a healthy, slimming meal.

Nuts and Seeds
Many people like to include nuts and seeds in their diet as snacks, but these foods tend to be high in fat content and therefore alarmingly high in calories.

The news is not all bad, though, as nuts and seeds do not contain any cholesterol and their fats are usually unsaturated. They also tend to be high in vitamins and minerals.

So eat them by all means, but — as always — it is advisable to exercise a little moderation, especially if you are trying not to put on any extra weight.

Cakes, Pastries, Crackers, Crispbreads
Cakes and pastries tend to be high in calories and fat and not of any great nutritional value. If you must eat cakes, it is always better to make your own rather than to eat store-bought ones. When you bake at home, you should always use a healthy, polyunsaturated oil rather than butter, and substitute egg whites for some of the yolks.

Read the labels on packages of crackers and crispbreads before you buy them, as they are often coated in vegetable

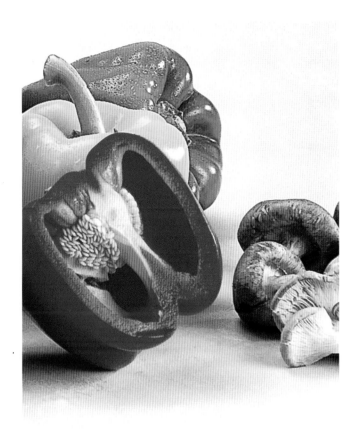

> ### RECOMMENDED NUTRIENT INTAKE
>
> **Total fat** 35% of total energy
> (E.g. in a 2,000 calorie diet, not more than 700 calories should come from fat. This equals 3 ounces (80 grams) fat per day, or 1^1/$_2$ ounces (40 grams) fat for every 1,000 calories.
> **Saturated fatty acids** Less than 10% of total energy
> **Polyunsaturated fatty acids** Up to 10% of total energy
> **Monounsaturated fatty acids** 10–15% of total energy
> **Carbohydrate** 50% of total calories
> **Protein** 10–20% of total calories
> **Total calories** Keep an eye on these in order to achieve and maintain your desirable weight

oil before crisping and may actually be much higher in fat than you think. Store-bought cookies and cakes are often rich in hidden fats, which are usually saturated, so again, read the labels carefully.

Choosing your foods

Nowadays, many of the foods that you will find on sale in the supermarkets are labeled with their carbohydrate, fat, protein, and calorie content. This is a very useful guide and it is therefore a good idea to get into the habit of studying food labels carefully. If you do this, it can then become automatic to calculate a recommended daily intake of all the main nutrient groups.

The recommended proportions of various nutrients are shown in the following table:

Cooking methods

Whenever possible, it is better to broil or bake than to fry foods, and to use no additional fat. If you do fry, make sure that you use an unsaturated oil rather than butter or lard, and cook in a nonstick skillet so that you need only the tiniest amount of oil in order to prevent the food from sticking.

Steaming and microwaving are also excellent methods of cooking. They are not only healthy, but they also retain a good deal of the flavor, texture, and color of the food, so that it also looks appetizing and appealing. On no account add any extra fat before, during, or after cooking, as this would defeat the whole purpose of the exercise of using this healthy cooking method.

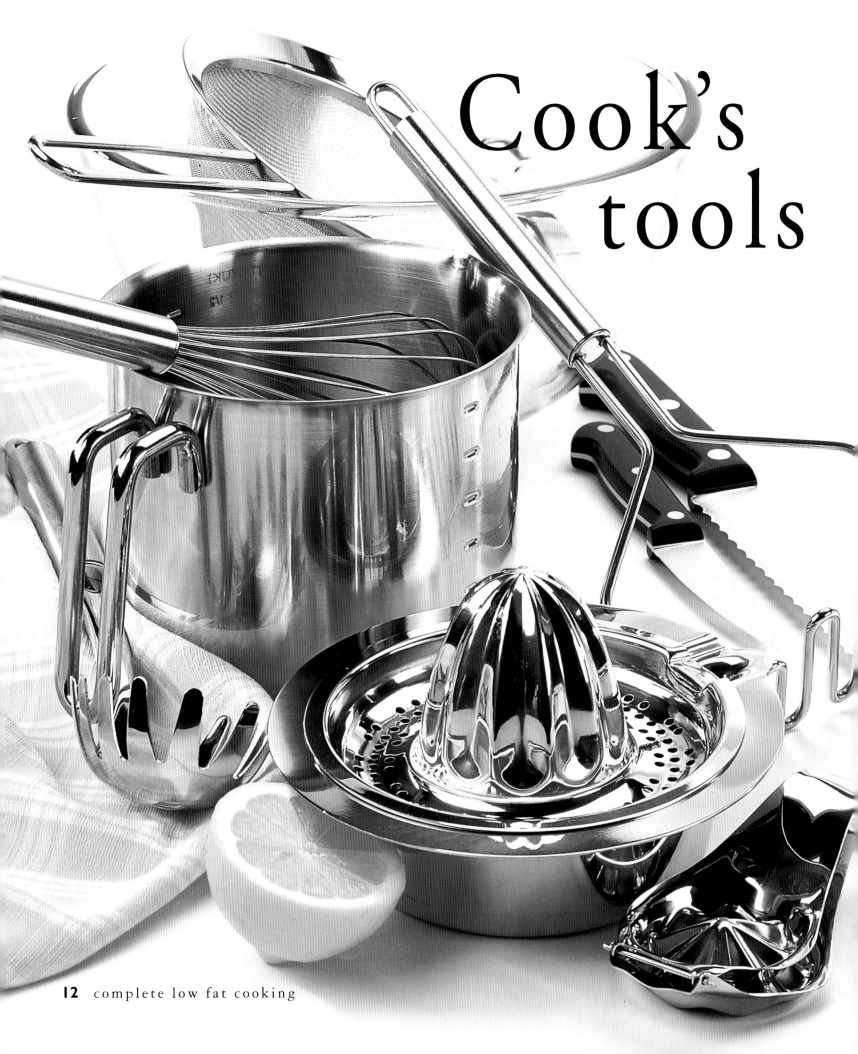

Cook's tools

"Give me neither poverty nor riches;
feed me with food convenient to me."

Proverbs 30:8

Mixing bowl

A mixing bowl should be wide enough to allow mixtures to be beaten or folded. The bowl should be rested on a grip stand or a cloth to prevent it slipping.

Sieve

A sieve has a rigid frame and a mesh dome in variations from fine to coarse. It can be used for separating solids from liquids, solids from solids, and also for refining ingredients. The mesh should be stainless steel to prevent rust.

Vegetable masher

A masher is used to mash cooked starchy vegetables, such as potatoes, yams, and carrots.

Whisk

A whisk is an essential beating tool used to blend ingredients and incorporate air into egg whites or liquid mixtures. Whisks come in different shapes and sizes — small ones are used for sauces, though the larger balloon whisk is the most popular and commonly used. They are very handy for rescuing a lumpy sauce.

Pasta server

A pasta server is a large spoon-shaped implement made of stainless steel or plastic with a long handle, used for transferring pasta or noodles from the pan to the serving dish. It has characteristic "teeth" which enable you to pick up spaghetti and fettucine easily, and a hole which lets the liquid drain away.

Lemon squeezers

Lemon squeezers are used for extracting the juice from a lemon and come in two shapes. One shape is designed to thoroughly remove the juice from half a lemon, while the other is used to squeeze lemon wedges. Lemon squeezers are made of stainless steel or plastic.

Knives

Every cook's most important tool is a set of sharp knives. The knives should be well maintained, cleaned and dried thoroughly after use, and sharpened regularly. Choose a set with smooth rather than serrated edges.

Garlic crusher

A garlic crusher is used to crush garlic finely by forcing the flesh through small holes. This releases the oils and the full flavor of the garlic. This useful tool prevents the pungent aroma of garlic from lingering on your skin, as you do not have to handle the garlic while crushing it.

Measuring cups

A measuring cup is a standardized measure of liquid. It should have a good pouring lip. These cups may be marked in metric and American liquid measurements, fractions of pints and fluid ounces, as well as milliliters and liters. Cups are available in glass, stainless steel, and plastic. Always check before buying a measuring cup that it is dishwasher proof.

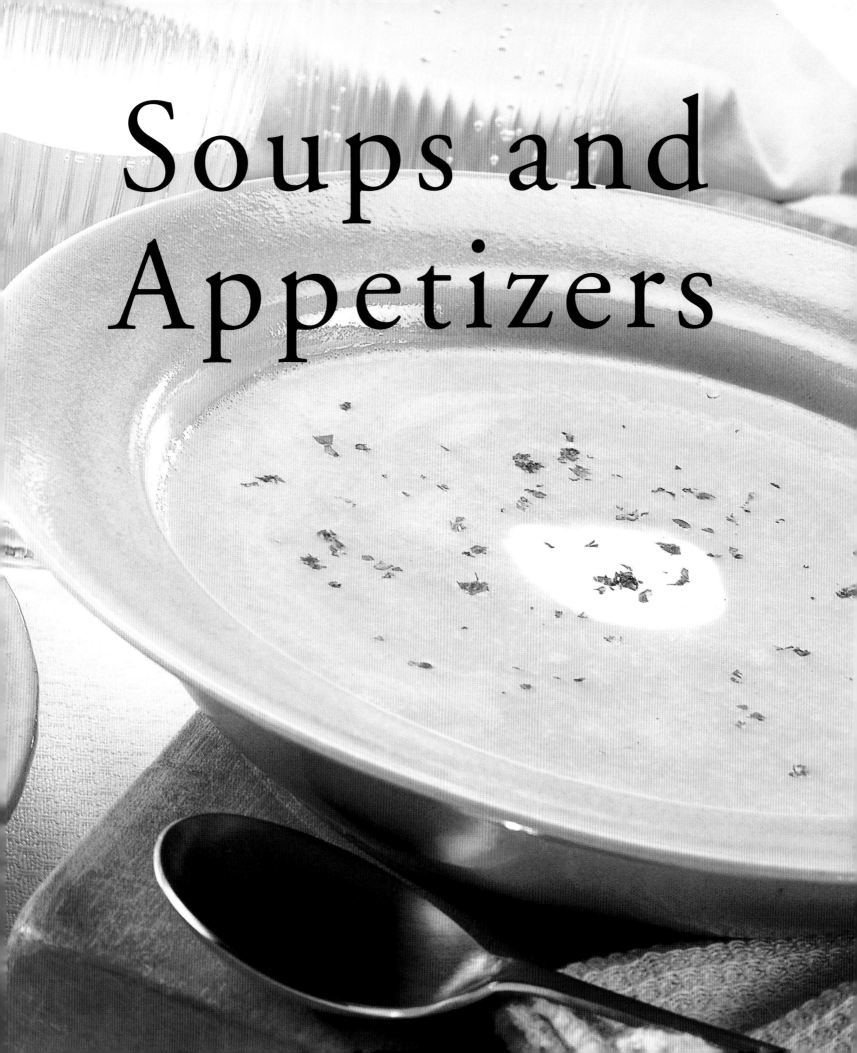

Soups and Appetizers

Celery Root and Apple Soup

2 tablespoons butter or margarine
1 celery root (about 1 pound), peeled and chopped
3 baking apples, peeled, cored, and chopped
5 cups Chicken or Vegetable Broth (see page 244)
pinch of cayenne pepper, or more to taste
salt and freshly ground white pepper

Garnish
2–3 tablespoons finely diced baking apple
paprika

melt the butter or margarine in a large saucepan and cook the celery root and apples over a moderate heat for 5 minutes or until the vegetables have begun to soften.

add the broth and cayenne pepper and bring to a boil. Lower the heat and simmer, covered, for 25–30 minutes, or until the celery root and apples are very soft.

purée the mixture in batches in a blender or food processor, until it is very smooth, transferring each successive batch to a clean saucepan. Reheat gently. Season to taste with salt and pepper. Serve hot in heated soup bowls or plates. Garnish each portion with the finely diced apple and a dusting of paprika.

Serves 6
Preparation time: *10–15 minutes*
Cooking time: *about 35 minutes*

protein 1 g • fat 4 g • cholest. 6 g

clipboard: Cayenne, or red pepper, is made from the dried and ground flesh and seeds of the bird's eye chili pepper. It is similar to chili powder but not usually as hot. Paprika is made from mild varieties of capsicum, or sweet pepper, whose seeds are removed before they are dried and ground. It should be bought in small quantities and not kept for long, as it loses both flavor and color remarkably quickly.

Rice Noodle Soup

3 cups Vegetable Broth (see page 244)
3 green onions (scallions), cut into 1 inch lengths
2 baby sweetcorn, sliced obliquely
1 tomato, quartered
1 onion, cut into 8 pieces
6 lime leaves, shredded
1 celery stick, chopped
½ cup ready-steamed tofu, diced
1 tablespoon soy sauce
1 teaspoon freshly ground black pepper
1–2 teaspoons crushed dried chili peppers
6 ounces dried wide rice noodles, soaked and drained

Garnish
fresh coriander (cilantro) leaves, cut into strips
lime quarters

heat the broth in a saucepan and add all of the ingredients except for the noodles.

bring to a boil for 30 seconds, then reduce the heat to a simmer, and cook for 5 minutes.

add the noodles and simmer for another 2 minutes.

pour into a serving bowl, garnish with coriander sprigs, and serve with lime quarters.

Serves 4
Preparation time: *10 minutes, plus 15–20 minutes soaking time*
Cooking time: *8 minutes*

protein 9 g • fat 3 g • cholest. 40 g

clipboard: Lime leaves give food an intensely citrus aroma. They can be bought dried, in which case half the quantity stated should be used, or fresh, which will keep for several weeks in the refrigerator. They are frequently used in Indonesian, Thai, and other southeast Asian dishes. Rice noodles are sold in packages at supermarkets and Chinese food stores. They cook quickly and are a particularly tasty and filling addition to a soup.

Green Garden Soup

This soup is a hearty broth made with a selection of fresh green vegetables — celery, leeks, watercress, lettuce, green onions (scallions), and fennel. It's as good for you as it is delicious to eat.

4 celery sticks, chopped

2 leeks, cleaned and chopped

I bunch of watercress, washed and chopped

I heart of a butter lettuce, shredded

4 green onions (scallions), chopped

I tablespoon chopped fresh tarragon

I garlic clove, peeled and crushed

I small head fennel, shredded

2½ cups Chicken Broth (see page 244)

1¼ cups skim milk

2 ounces fine green fettucine, broken into short lengths

salt and freshly ground black pepper

put the celery, leeks, watercress, lettuce, green onions (scallions), tarragon, garlic, and fennel into a large pan; add the broth, skimmed milk and salt and pepper to taste.

simmer the soup for 20–25 minutes until all the vegetables are tender.

blend the soup in a blender until smooth.

return the soup to a clean pan and bring to a boil. Add the broken fettucine and simmer for about 4 minutes, until the pasta is just tender. Serve the soup piping hot.

Serves 4
Preparation time: *15 minutes*
Cooking time: *about 30 minutes*

protein 8 g • fat 1 g • cholest. 18 g

Chilled Pea Soup

A chilled soup is always a refreshingly welcome dish to serve in the summer months, when the weather is hot. This lemony pea soup, garnished with chopped fresh mint, is just the ticket.

3 cups fresh shelled peas or frozen petit pois
I cup diced potatoes
I onion, minced
I large sprig of mint
finely grated rind of ½ lemon
2 tablespoons lemon juice
3¾ cups Chicken Broth (see page 244)
salt and pepper
I tablespoon chopped fresh mint, to garnish

place the peas in a large saucepan with the potatoes, onion, mint sprig, lemon rind and juice, and broth, and season with salt and pepper. Bring to a boil, lower heat, cover and simmer for 15–20 minutes or until the peas are tender.

purée in a blender or press through a sieve. Set aside to cool.

adjust the seasoning to taste and chill in the refrigerator for 2–3 hours. Serve chilled, sprinkled with the mint.

Serves 4
Preparation time: *20 minutes, plus chilling*
Cooking time: *15–20 minutes*

protein 6 g • fat 1 g • cholest. 18 g

clipboard: Mint is one of the most popular herbs for use in the kitchen. It is a member of the same family as sage, thyme, marjoram, oregano, rosemary, basil, savory, and lemon balm. The flavor combines particularly well with peas and potatoes, both of which are used in this recipe.

Salad leaves

Chinese (Napa) cabbage

Arugula   *Little Gem*   *Leaf*

Chinese (Napa) cabbage

This pale green cabbage with tightly packed leaves which form a long, thin, tapering cabbage originates from southeast Asia. The leaves have a clean delicate flavor and can be used as a steamed vegetable or in salads and stir-fries.

Arugula

Originally from Europe, arugula was a popular kitchen herb in Colonial America (when it was known as rocket) and has recently enjoyed a great revival in popularity. It has a slightly peppery flavor and can be eaten raw or added to pasta dishes.

Little Gem

Little Gem is a small loose-leaved lettuce, which has crisp, slightly crinkled little leaves in a pale green color. It is of more interest for its crispness than its flavor, which is rather bland. It is a popular salad green, and also makes a good garnish. It has a crisp heart.

Leaf

Leaf lettuce is a crisp, fresh, pale green lettuce with loose, curly leaves, which is used either in a green salad or as a garnish. It has good keeping qualities and will last well for several days in the salad drawer of the refrigerator.

Radicchio

Lamb's lettuce (Mâche)

Endive

Chicory

Radicchio

The crisp, dark pinkish red leaves with their white ribs look absolutely wonderful in a salad, especially when combined with other salad greens. They have a distinctive flavor and make an attractive garnish. They can also be broiled or fried.

Lamb's lettuce

Also known as corn salad or mâche, lamb's lettuce has a pleasantly mild, slightly nutty flavor and is excellent in salads, either on its own or in combination with other salad greens. Its delicate little leaves look good when used as a garnish, too.

Endive

Also known as Belgian endive or witloof, this is a compact cone-shaped salad vegetable with long, slightly crisp, yellow-tipped leaves. It can be cooked or used in salads, too. The roots are also roasted, ground and are sometimes added to coffee.

Chicory

Also known as curly endive or frisée. It has attractive lacy leaves in various shades of green, yellow, and even white. It is a member of the endive family and has a slightly bitter taste. It makes an attractive garnish, too.

Italian Leek and Pumpkin Soup

The hollowed-out shell of the pumpkin can be used to make an impressive tureen in which to serve this soup.

1 Bermuda onion, chopped

1 leek, white parts only, chopped

2½ cups hot Chicken Broth (see page 244)

4 cups pumpkin flesh

2 medium potatoes

2½ cups skim milk

½ cup cooked long-grain rice

⅔ cup plain low-fat yogurt

salt and freshly ground black pepper

chopped parsley, to garnish

soften the onion and leek in 2 tablespoons of the broth. Dice the pumpkin flesh and potatoes and add, with the salt and pepper, the milk, and the remaining broth, to the onions. Bring to a boil, cover and simmer for 45 minutes, stirring frequently.

blend the soup in a blender or press through a sieve. Return to the pan, and add the cooked rice and most of the yogurt. Reheat gently. Serve, topped with the remaining yogurt and sprinkled with parsley.

Serves 8
Preparation time: *30 minutes*
Cooking time: *45 minutes*

protein 5 g • fat 1 g • cholest. 16 g

clipboard: Pumpkin has a golden, nutty-flavored flesh and a center filled with edible seeds. There are numerous varieties, which can be served steamed, boiled, baked, and stuffed.

French Onion Soup

French onion soup is a classic recipe, which is traditionally served with its characteristic slices of toasted bread and cheese on top.

3 large Bermuda onions, minced
5 cups beef broth, made with 2 broth cubes
1 teaspoon sugar
6 slices French bread
4 ounces reduced-fat Jack cheese, shredded
1 tablespoon brandy
salt and freshly ground black pepper
chopped parsley, to garnish (optional)

cook the onions in some of the broth in a heavy-bottomed covered pan for at least 30 minutes, stirring frequently. They should not brown but should be quite soft. Add the rest of the broth, the sugar, salt and pepper, and simmer for a further 30 minutes.

meanwhile, toast the bread slices in the oven, heap the shredded cheese on top and brown under the broiler. Now stir the brandy into the soup and serve with a toasted bread slice in each bowl. Sprinkle with chopped parsley, if desired.

Serves 6
Preparation time: *20 minutes*
Cooking time: *1 hour*

protein 8 g • fat 3 g • cholest. 16 g

Fresh Tomato Soup

This recipe for tomato soup is not only simple, it is also delicious. The subtle orange flavor really does make all the difference to this popular soup.

2 pounds ripe tomatoes, roughly chopped

I small onion, chopped

I tablespoon vegetable oil

I sugar cube

I orange

6½ cups Chicken or Vegetable Broth
(see page 244)

2 cloves

bouquet garni

fresh thyme leaves, to garnish

soften the tomatoes and onion in the oil for about 8 minutes. Rub the sugar cube over the orange rind, to absorb the zest, and add with the remaining ingredients to the tomato mixture. Bring to a boil, cover, and simmer gently for 25 minutes. Remove the cloves and bouquet garni.

blend the soup in a blender, then push with a wooden spoon through a fine sieve. Reheat and serve, garnished with thyme leaves.

Serves 8
Preparation time: *20 minutes*
Cooking time: *35 minutes*

protein 2 g • fat 2 g • cholest. 7 g

clipboard: A bouquet garni usually consists of a bayleaf, a sprig of thyme, and 3 stalks of parsley. It is often enclosed in a piece of celery stick or a piece of leek, tied with string, or it can be wrapped in a small square of cheesecloth, tied with thin string or thread.

Young Vegetables
with Garlic Sauce

Use an adventurous selection of seasonal vegetables: steamed young zucchini, carrots, baby sweetcorn, white cabbage, cauliflower, and mushrooms. Cold new potatoes in their skins taste especially good with the garlic sauce. Lightly steam the vegetables or leave them raw, according to taste.

about 9 cups raw and/or cooked vegetables

Sauce
3–4 large garlic cloves, peeled and roughly chopped
1 teaspoon salt
2–3 tablespoons lemon juice
4 tablespoons tahini (sesame seed paste)
1 teaspoon olive oil
2 teaspoons finely chopped fresh parsley
or coriander
freshly ground black pepper

prepare the vegetables, trimming and steaming, as necessary.

make the sauce. Using a pestle and mortar, grind the garlic to a pulp with the salt, then add the lemon juice.

slowly incorporate the mixture into the tahini, adding enough water to make a consistency similar to that of thick cream.

taste and adjust the seasoning with salt, pepper or lemon juice. Finally stir in the oil and parsley or coriander. Transfer to a small bowl.

arrange the vegetables on a platter. Serve with the garlic sauce on the side for easy dipping.

Serves 8
Preparation time: *about 30 minutes*
Cooking time: *according to vegetables*

protein 4 g • fat 5 g • cholest. 6 g

Smoked Chicken

with Peach Purée

3 ripe peaches
3 tablespoons dry vermouth
1 teaspoon French mustard
1 teaspoon chopped fresh tarragon
12 thin slices smoked chicken
salt and freshly ground black pepper

Garnish
thin slices of fresh peach
small sprigs of fresh tarragon

nick the stalk end of each peach. Plunge into a bowl of boiling water for 45 seconds, then slide off the skins. Pit the peaches and chop the flesh.

blend the peach flesh in a blender with the vermouth, mustard, chopped tarragon, and a little salt and pepper.

cover the sauce and chill for 1 hour. (Do not chill any longer in order to avoid discoloration.)

spoon a little of the sauce onto each plate, and lay 3 slices of chicken in a fan shape close by.

garnish with thin slices of peach and with sprigs of fresh tarragon.

Serves 4
Preparation time: *25 minutes, plus chilling*

protein 15 g • fat 3 g • cholest. 7 g

clipboard: Tarragon has a special affinity with chicken. French tarragon has a strong, clear flavor. Tarragon is easy to grow from cuttings, but it should be lifted every year and planted in a fresh spot, as it uses up all the trace elements in the soil and the flavor will therefore deteriorate.

Stuffed Grape Leaves

These grape leaves are filled with a delicious combination of chicken livers, rice, and pine nuts. Grape leaves can be bought canned or in packages.

2 teaspoons vegetable oil

I medium onion, peeled and chopped

I clove garlic, crushed

3 ounces chicken livers

½ cup cooked rice

2 tablespoons pine nuts

36 canned or packaged vine leaves

about 1¼ cups Chicken Broth (see page 244)

salt and freshly ground black pepper

heat the oil in a skillet and fry the onion and garlic until soft and transparent. Add the chicken livers and fry for a further 3 minutes, stirring constantly, until lightly browned on all sides. Remove the livers from the pan and chop finely. Place the rice in a bowl and add the livers, onion, garlic, and pan juices, the pine nuts, and salt and pepper to taste. Mix well.

lay the grape leaves on a work surface with the underside of the leaves face up. Put a teaspoon of the rice mixture on each leaf and roll them up, tucking the sides in, as for a burrito, to make a neat parcel. Place the leaves close together in a casserole, making two or more layers.

pour in enough broth to come halfway up the sides of the casserole and just cover the vine leaves. Cover and place in a preheated moderate oven at 350°F for 30–40 minutes until cooked through. Serve at once, or leave until cold.

Serves 6–8
Preparation time: *30 minutes*
Cooking time: *30–40 minutes*
Oven temperature: *350°F*

protein 7 g • fat 5 g • cholest. 7 g

Bean and Mushroom Salad

4 cups frozen whole green beans
4 cups button mushrooms
juice of ½ lemon
½ small onion, grated
a little ground coriander (cilantro)
3 tablespoons chopped parsley
1¼ cups Low-Calorie French
Dressing (see page 246)
salt

cook the beans in boiling salted water until just tender, then cool under running water. Drain thoroughly.

wipe the mushrooms with a clean damp cloth and slice finely. Sprinkle with lemon juice. Add the onion, ground coriander (cilantro) and parsley to the French dressing, then pour this over the mushrooms. Leave to marinate for 1 or 2 hours, turning gently from time to time.

toss the mushroom mixture carefully with the green beans and serve in a large serving dish or on individual plates.

Serves 8
Preparation time: *10 minutes, plus 1 or 2 hours marinating*
Cooking time: *8–15 minutes*

protein 4 g • fat 1 g • cholest. 9 g

clipboard: green beans and mushrooms are a particularly successful combination. Fresh beans may be used instead of frozen ones, if you prefer.

Salads

Glass Noodle Salad

7 ounces dried glass noodles, soaked and drained

1 tomato, halved and sliced

1 celery stick, chopped

1 green onion (scallion), chopped

1 onion, halved and sliced

1 green bell pepper, cored, seeded and chopped

juice of 2 limes

5 small green chili peppers, finely chopped

2 teaspoons sugar

4 tablespoons crushed roasted peanuts

1 teaspoon crushed dried chili peppers

½ teaspoon salt

2½ teaspoons *nam pla* or fish sauce

fresh coriander (cilantro) sprigs, to garnish

cook the noodles in boiling water for 3–4 minutes, then drain and rinse them under cold water to prevent further cooking.

cut the noodles into 5-inch lengths. Return them to the pan and add all the remaining ingredients. Mix thoroughly for 2 minutes.

serve at room temperature, garnished with fresh coriander sprigs.

Serves 4
Preparation time: *15 minutes, plus soaking*
Cooking time: *3–4 minutes*

protein 9 g • fat 4 g • cholest. 44 g

clipboard: To make crushed roasted peanuts, dry-fry the nuts in a skillet until they turn a golden color, then allow to cool. Place them in a plastic bag and break into small pieces using a rolling pin. *Nam pla* is a salty, spiced, fermented fish mixture, and is available from Oriental food stores and some supermarkets.

Mushroom, Zucchini, and Tomato Salad

6 large mushrooms, sliced
4 zucchini, thinly sliced
4 tomatoes, peeled and quartered
1 teaspoon chopped fresh basil
1 bunch watercress, trimmed, and divided into sprigs
3 tablespoons Low-Calorie French Dressing (see page 246), to serve

combine the mushrooms, zucchini, and tomatoes in a salad bowl and sprinkle with the basil.

arrange the sprigs of watercress around the edge of the salad. Serve with the dressing.

Serves 4
Preparation time: *15 minutes*

protein 3 g • fat 1 g • cholest. 8 g

clipboard: A combination of contrasting colors gives a salad visual appeal and makes the mouth water in anticipation. Mushrooms, zucchini, and tomatoes not only look good together, they also complement each other in taste.

Provençal Pasta Salad

6 ounces rigatoni or penne
4 tablespoons Low-Calorie French Dressing
(see page 246)
juice of ½ lemon
6 tomatoes, skinned, seeded, and chopped
⅔ cup green beans, cooked
12 black olives, pitted
1 cup canned tuna in brine, drained and flaked
salt and freshly ground black pepper
1 x 2 ounce can anchovy fillets, drained and washed,
to garnish
1 small head Boston lettuce, shredded, to serve

bring a large saucepan of salted water to a boil. Add the pasta, stir and cook for 10–12 minutes, until *al dente*. Drain the pasta well and mix with a little of the dressing.

allow the pasta to cool, turn it into a bowl, and mix with the lemon juice, tomatoes, beans, olives, and flaked tuna. Season with salt and pepper.

toss the salad lightly in the remaining dressing and serve on a bed of shredded lettuce. Garnish with anchovies.

Serves 6
Preparation time: *10–12 minutes,*
  plus cooling
Cooking time: *about 12 minutes*

protein 14 g • fat 5 g • cholest. 26 g

Apple and Walnut Salad

Salads made with fruits and nuts make a refreshing change from the usual salad ingredients and add an interesting variation in texture as well as flavor.

1 iceberg lettuce, sliced
2 bunches watercress, trimmed and chopped
1 apple, peeled, cubed and tossed in lemon juice
2 tablespoons walnuts, chopped
1 tablespoon walnut oil
2 tablespoons wine vinegar
salt and freshly ground black pepper

mix the lettuce with the watercress and apple.

sprinkle the walnuts over and drizzle on the walnut oil and vinegar. Season with salt and pepper. Toss the salad well just before serving.

Serves 6
Preparation time: *15–20 minutes*

protein 2 g • fat 5 g • cholest. 3 g

clipboard: The partnership of apples with walnuts was made in heaven, but other fruit and nut combinations can work equally well. In the summer months, try peach and almonds with almond oil, for example, or apricots and almonds.

Tricolor Salad

Bright colors and contrasting textures make this salad a refreshing antidote to the end of winter. For the best flavor, serve at room temperature, not chilled.

1 large leek, trimmed and sliced into rings
2 red bell peppers, cored, seeded and diced
2 medium oranges, about ½ cup flesh, peeled, sliced, slices cut into quarters
1 tablespoon chopped fresh dill
1 tablespoon chopped fresh parsley
⅔ pint plain low-fat yogurt
1 teaspoon clear honey
freshly ground black pepper
sprig of fresh dill, to garnish

combine the prepared leeks, red pepper, and oranges in individual bowls or a serving dish.

blend together the dill, parsley, yogurt, honey, and pepper and pour over the salad. Garnish with the sprig of dill.

Serves 4
Preparation time: *10 minutes*

protein 3 g • fat 1 g • cholest. 12 g

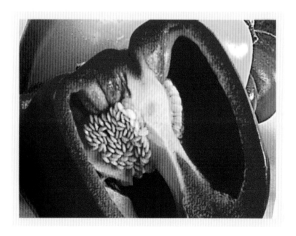

clipboard: Dill is a rather tall herb which grows up to 2 feet high. It has hollow stems, thin thread-like leaves and umbels of yellow flowers. It looks very similar to fennel. It goes particularly well with fish and in soups, cream sauces, salads, vegetable dishes, and pickles.

Spanish Coleslaw

This is coleslaw with a difference, with the addition of green and red bell peppers and grapes. It's a colorful salad, which looks as good as it tastes.

2 cups finely shredded white cabbage
I small onion, minced
½ green pepper, cored, seeded and chopped
½ red pepper, cored, seeded and chopped
I large carrot, grated
¼ cup grapes
6 tablespoons natural low-fat yogurt
I tablespoon Low-calorie French Dressing
(see page 246)
salt and freshly ground black pepper
chopped parsley, to garnish

place the cabbage in a bowl and add the onion, green and red peppers, carrot, and grapes.

mix together the yogurt and dressing. Season with salt and pepper to taste. Add to the vegetables and toss thoroughly. Transfer to a serving bowl and garnish with chopped parsley.

Serves 4
Preparation time: *20 minutes*

protein 4 g • fat 1 g • cholest. 12 g

Herbs and Spices

Dill

Chervil

Rosemary

Basil

Thyme

Marjoram

Dill
Dill also known as dillweed is an annual herb from Europe and grows to about 2 feet. It has hollow stems, feathery thread-like leaves, umbels of yellow flowers, and seeds that look rather like caraway or cumin seeds. The plant looks almost identical to fennel. The seeds are believed to aid the digestion. Dill goes well with fish and is also used in soups, sauces, pickles, and salads.

Basil
Basil is a delicious summer herb with an intense aroma and a distinctive flavor. It is used extensively in Greek and Italian cooking and is the main ingredient in pesto sauce, the basil-flavored sauce often served with pasta. Basil also has a great affinity with tomatoes. It loses flavor when cooked, so it is added to dishes at the end of cooking, used as a garnish, or added to cold dishes such as salads.

Chervil
Chervil originated in the Middle East and southern Russia and was probably introduced into Europe by the Romans. It is a biennial plant growing to about 16 inches, with fern-like leaves and small white flowers with little black seed pods. It is especially tasty in soups, with chicken, fish, salads, and eggs. It is best added once the cooking is over as it does not respond well to heat.

Thyme
Thyme is a bushy shrub with gray-green leaves and pink, mauve, red, or white flowers. It has a fragrant aroma and a clove-like flavor. It can be bought fresh or dried, combines well with other herbs, and can withstand long cooking.

Rosemary
Rosemary is a perennial herb with long spiky green leaves and pale blue flowers. It can be bought fresh or dried, and is also easy to cultivate at home. When it is fresh, it is strongly flavored, and aromatic. It is often used to flavor vinegars and oils.

Marjoram
Sweet marjoram, the more commonly used variety, has a warm, delicate flavor and goes well with tomatoes and in pasta, chicken, and vegetable dishes. It is best added at the end of the cooking time.

Nutmeg

Root ginger

Lemongrass

Saffron

Chili peppers

Kaffir lime leaves

Saffron

Made from the dried stigmas of the crocus plant, saffron is the most expensive of all spices. It is available either as whole threads or ground into a powder. The threads are generally considered to be stronger.

Nutmeg

The nutmeg tree originally grew in the Molucca Islands, where it was an important constituent of the spice trade. The seed of the tree grows within a lacy cage of mace and is dried in the sun after harvesting. It is sold both whole and ground but is best bought whole and grated into milk-based puddings, sauces, vegetable dishes, and fruit cakes.

Chili peppers

Chili peppers are extremely fiery and must therefore be used with caution. Removing the seeds tones down some of their heat. Be careful to wash your hands after handling chili peppers and never touch your eyes. Dried red chili peppers are available whole, crushed, or flaked. There are hundreds of varieties

Root ginger

A thick knobby root with pale brown skin and moist pale-gold flesh, this has a slightly hot, pungent flavor. It is an essential ingredient in East Indian and Southeast Asian cooking. Dried and ground, ginger can also be used to give a kick to cakes, cookies, and desserts.

Lemongrass

In its fresh state, lemongrass is considered to be an herb, but when it is dried, whether whole or powdered, it is considered to be a spice. The flavor is reminiscent of lemon rind, and it is an important ingredient in southeast Asian cuisine. The whole dried stem should be soaked before being used in cooking, whereas the powdered kind does not require soaking and is therefore easier to use.

Kaffir lime leaves

Strongly citrus-flavored, these are available fresh or dried in Oriental food stores and markets, and are used in southeast Asian cookery. Kaffir limes are grown mainly as ornamental and dooryard trees in the United States. Key lime or lemon leaves may be used as a substitute, fresh or dried.

complete low fat cooking **57**

Brown Rice and Mixed Herb Salad

1 small onion, peeled and minced
1 garlic clove, peeled and minced
½ teaspoon garam masala
⅔ cup long-grain brown rice
pinch of powdered saffron
1¾ cups Chicken Broth (see page 244)
½ tablespoon unsweetened shredded coconut
2 teaspoons olive oil
2 tablespoons tarragon vinegar
1 tablespoon chopped fresh coriander (cilantro)
2 tablespoons chopped fresh parsley
10 cashew nuts, lightly toasted
salt and freshly ground black pepper

dry-fry the onion gently for 3 minutes; add the garlic, garam masala, and rice, and fry gently for a further 2 minutes, stirring continuously.

stir in the saffron, chicken broth, shredded coconut, salt and pepper to taste. Bring to a boil and simmer gently for about 25 minutes, until the rice is just tender.

mix the olive oil with the tarragon vinegar, the coriander (cilantro), and parsley, and season to taste. Stir evenly through the warm rice, together with the cashew nuts.

allow to cool before serving.

Serves 4
Preparation time: *10 minutes, plus chilling*
Cooking time: *30–35 minutes*

protein 4 g • fat 5 g • cholest. 33 g

clipboard: The quality of brown rice varies enormously and some types absorb more liquid while cooking than others, so check from time to time to see that the rice is not becoming too dry and, if necessary, add some extra chicken stock. Garam masala is a traditional Indian spice mixture, which is available ready-prepared. It usually includes cardamom, cloves, cinnamon, black pepper, and perhaps nutmeg.

Vegetables

Artichokes Provençal

For such an ugly-looking vegetable, Jerusalem artichokes have a surprisingly delicate flavor. They are in season in winter and spring and are very nutritious, being rich in phosphorus and potassium.

2 pounds Jerusalem artichokes, scraped
2 large garlic cloves, crushed
4 tomatoes, skinned, seeded, and chopped
2 tablespoons tomato paste
juice of ½ lemon
1 tablespoon chopped fresh basil
or ½ teaspoon dried basil
1 teaspoon sugar
2 tablespoons chopped parsley
salt and freshly ground black pepper

slice the artichokes thickly and steam or poach them for about 20 minutes until tender.

meanwhile, mix the garlic and the tomatoes and cook for about 10 minutes, stirring frequently, until the liquid has reduced a little. When the texture is pulpy, add the tomato paste, lemon juice, basil, sugar, salt, and pepper. Heat through and pour over the cooked artichokes in a serving dish. Just before serving, sprinkle with chopped parsley. This dish is equally delicious served hot or cold.

Serves 6
Preparation time: *20 minutes*
Cooking time: *30 minutes*

protein 4 g • fat 0 g • cholest. 22 g

Scalloped Potatoes

2 teaspoons vegetable oil
⅓ cup low-fat sour cream
1½ cup skimmed milk
2 tablespoons low-fat spread
1 tablespoon cornstarch
⅛ teaspoon pepper
4 medium potatoes,
cut into ¼ inch slices
½ medium onion, diced
paprika, to taste
sprigs of thyme, to serve

brush a rectangular 8 inch x 5 inch baking dish with oil.

in a medium bowl, whisk together the sour cream, skim milk, low-fat spread, cornstarch, and pepper.

line the dish with one-third of the potato slices. Pour one-third of the sour cream mixture over the potatoes. Sprinkle half of the onion over the sour cream mixture. Repeat the layers in order: one-third of the potatoes, one-third of the sour cream mixture, and the remaining onion. Arrange the remaining potatoes on the top and pour the remaining sour cream mixture over the top. Cover with foil and bake in a preheated oven at 350°F for 1 hour. Remove the foil and bake for a further 20 minutes.

sprinkle with paprika and thyme sprigs, then let stand for 5 minutes before serving.

Serves 6
Preparation time: *20 minutes*
Cooking time: *1 hour 20 minutes*
Oven temperature: *350°F*

protein 5 g • fat 5 g • cholest. 30 g

Pan-braised Peppers *with Tomato*

This delicious dish, full of flavor and color, is suitable for vegetarians.

1 tablespoon vegetable oil
2 medium onions, coarsely chopped
3 large bell peppers, red, green and yellow, cored, seeded and cut into strips
4 tomatoes, skinned and chopped
1 teaspoon coriander (cilantro) seeds
1 teaspoon black peppercorns
½ teaspoon salt
½ teaspoon chili powder

heat the oil in a large skillet and fry the onions for about 5 minutes, until golden. Add the peppers and cook gently for 2–3 minutes, then stir in the tomatoes.

crush the coriander (cilantro) seeds and peppercorns. Use a pestle and mortar if you have one, otherwise put the seeds and peppercorns between double sheets of paper towels and crush with a rolling pin. Add the salt and chili powder to the crushed seeds and sprinkle the mixture over the peppers and tomatoes. Mix together lightly, cover the pan, and cook gently for 20 minutes. This can be prepared up to 24 hours in advance and kept covered in the refrigerator.

Serves 4
Preparation time: *25 minutes*
Cooking time: *28 minutes*

protein 3 g • fat 4 g • cholest. 14 g

clipboard: It is not essential to use different-colored peppers, but it does look attractive. This dish is wonderful served hot and almost as good served cold with a salad selection.

Raw Vegetables
with Yellow Bean Sauce

Good vegetables to choose for this dish are peeled broccoli stalks, carrot, cucumber, and zucchini, cooked green beans, Chinese (Napa) cabbage, cauliflower flowerets, and bell pepper strips.

about 6 cups vegetables of your choice
1 red California or Anaheim chili pepper, sliced lengthwise, to garnish

Yellow Bean Sauce
½ cup yellow beans
½ onion, chopped
1 tablespoon tamarind water
1 cup coconut milk
1 cup water
2 eggs
3 tablespoons sugar
1 tablespoon soy sauce

choose a mixture of raw vegetables and chop them into sticks if necessary.

make the sauce: blend the yellow beans and the onion in a blender or food processor and pour into a saucepan. Add the rest of the sauce ingredients and bring gradually to a boil, stirring. Remove from the heat and pour into a bowl.

garnish the prepared sauce with the red chili pepper and serve warm, with the vegetables.

Serves 4 as a vegetarian main course
Preparation time: *15 minutes*
Cooking time: *5–6 minutes*

protein 7 g • fat 4 g • cholest. 24 g

clipboard: Tamarind refers to the dried pods of the tamarind, or Indian date. These are sour tasting and need to be soaked in hot water to extract the flavor. Tamarind can be bought as a paste in jars and needs to be mixed with a little water to bring it to a liquid consistency. Lemon is often used as a substitute, though tamarind has a much stronger flavor.

Summer Vegetables
with Yogurt and Mint

1 cup fava beans (weighed without pods)
2 cups green beans, strings removed and sliced
2 cups fresh garden peas (weighed without pods)
⅔ cup plain low-fat yogurt
1 tablespoon chopped fresh mint
salt and freshly ground black pepper

cook the fava beans for about 8 minutes in a little boiling, salted water, then drain thoroughly.

cook the green beans and peas together for 5 minutes in boiling water and drain thoroughly.

heat the yogurt very gently in one of the vegetable pans, add the vegetables, and toss to coat thoroughly. Gently stir in the mint and black pepper to taste, and serve.

Serves 4
Preparation time: *25 minutes*
Cooking time: *15 minutes*

protein 11 g • fat 1 g • cholest. 17 g

clipboard: Fava beans originated in Persia and Africa, and have been used in European — especially Mediterranean — cuisine for centuries. The beans must be shelled and the tough outer skin should be removed before cooking.

Vegetables

Pumpkin

Carrots

Celery root

Jerusalem artichokes

Jerusalem artichokes

This is a native American vegetable, which is not in fact an artichoke at all but a tuber of a species of sunflower. The word "Jerusalem" derives from *girasole*, which is Italian for sunflower. Jerusalem artichokes can be eaten raw in salads, or cooked like potatoes as a side-dish. They make a particularly delicious soup.

Carrots

Long root vegetables with sweet orange flesh, carrots are highly nutritious, particularly when they are eaten raw. They can also be cooked in casseroles or served as an accompanying vegetable.

Celery Root

This swollen knobby root of a variety of celery has a firm, crisp white flesh, and a flavor similar to that of celery. It may be grated and eaten raw in salads, or cooked in soups, stews and casseroles. It is at its best in winter.

Pumpkin

The pumpkin is a member of the gourd family. It has a slightly bland flesh, but is delicious in well-flavored soups, stews, and pies. There are many varieties.

Celery

Bell peppers

Shiitake
mushrooms

Oyster
mushrooms

Red cabbage

Red cabbage
Cabbage— both green and red— is a highly nutritious vegetable with tightly packed leaves. It can be served as an accompanying vegetable with meat or fish, or eaten raw in salads. Red cabbage is available all year round and is relatively inexpensive.

Celery
A long crisp stalk, celery is most commonly used either in salads, when it gives a welcome crunchiness, or it can be cooked as an accompanying vegetable or served in soups, casseroles, and stews. It is available all year round and is relatively inexpensive.

Bell peppers
Green, red, golden, purple, and yellow bell peppers add color and texture to salads, or are used in soups, stews, and stir-fries. They are rich in vitamin C.

Mushrooms
Possibly one of the oldest plants in the world, mushrooms are available all year round. There are some 250 different varieties of wild and cultivated mushrooms, including oyster and shiitake mushrooms. Shiitake mushrooms have a fragrant, golden brown cap, which is often dried as this makes their flavor stronger.

Broiled Zucchini

with Mustard

1 pound zucchini, cut in half lengthwise
1 tablespoon butter or vegetable margarine, melted
1 tablespoon wholegrain mustard

brush the zucchini lightly with the melted butter and place them, cut-side downward, on a heated broiler pan or on a griddle. Broil under high heat until lightly browned.

turn them over and spread with the mustard. Broil until golden. Serve hot as an appetizer or an accompanying vegetable.

Serves 4
Preparation time: *10 minutes*
Cooking time: *10 minutes*

protein 2 g • fat 4 g • cholest. 5 g

Broccoli Dressed

with Lemon

4 cups fresh broccoli
1 teaspoon olive oil
2 very thin strips of lemon rind, about
1½ inches long
2 tablespoons lemon juice
generous pinch of grated nutmeg
salt and freshly ground black pepper

trim most of the stalk off the broccoli heads. Peel the stalks and slice them thinly, diagonally. Wash the heads and break into small flowerets.

steam the broccoli heads for 8 minutes, then taste to see if they are done; they should still have some bite.

while the heads are steaming, cook the stalks. Heat the oil in a wok or large skillet until very hot, add the lemon rind, and stir-fry it until it starts to brown, then quickly add the sliced stalks. Stir-fry for barely 1 minute, then add the lemon juice, nutmeg, salt and pepper to taste, and fry for a further 30 seconds.

place the steamed flowerets in a serving dish and lay the stalks on top. Stir once, then leave to cool a little.

serve while still warm.

Serves 6
Preparation time: *20 minutes*
Cooking time: *10 minutes, plus standing time*

protein 7 g • fat 2 g • cholest. 3 g

clipboard: Nutmeg is the seed of the nutmeg tree and is dried in the sun after harvesting. It is sold either whole or ground, and is better bought whole and freshly grated, as the ground form quickly loses its spicy aroma.

Root Vegetable Bake

4 cups new potatoes, washed
2 cups yellow turnips, peeled and cubed
2 parsnips, peeled and sliced
4 carrots, peeled and cut into sticks
5 tablespoons Vegetable Broth (see page 244)
4 tablespoons reduced-fat yellow cheese
salt and freshly ground black pepper

Garnish
tomato slices
1 tablespoon chopped fresh parsley

preheat the oven to 350°F.

place the potatoes in a pan of boiling salted water and cook until just tender. Cut into ¼ inch slices. Place the remaining vegetables together in a large pan of salted water and bring to a boil. Boil until just tender. Drain all the vegetables and place in layers in a deep ovenproof dish, finishing with a border of overlapping potato slices. Pour the broth over them, sprinkle with the cheese, and season with pepper.

bake in the preheated oven at 350°F for 15–20 minutes or until the cheese has melted and the vegetables are heated through. Brown under a moderate broiler to finish, if wished.

serve garnished with tomato slices and chopped parsley.

Serves 4
Preparation time: *20 minutes*
Cooking time: *about 40–50 minutes*
Oven temperature: 350°F

protein 8 g • fat 3 g • cholest. 34 g

clipboard: An alternative is to cover the top completely with potato slices. Diced broiled bacon may be added before baking, but this will, of course, add to the fat content.

Pumpkin Curry

4 tablespoons grated fresh coconut

1¼ cups coconut water (from a fresh coconut)

2 tablespoons vegetable oil

1 onion, chopped

1 green bell pepper, cored, seeded and chopped

4 garlic cloves, crushed

2 slices fresh root ginger, peeled and finely chopped

¼ teaspoon turmeric

2 fresh green chili peppers, seeded and minced

¼ teaspoon ground cloves

¼ teaspoon crushed chili flakes

3 cups pumpkin, peeled, seeded and cut into 1 inch cubes

2 tomatoes, skinned and chopped

salt and freshly ground black pepper

put the grated fresh coconut in a bowl and add the coconut water. You can drain this out of a fresh coconut by piercing it a couple of times with a skewer and draining out the liquid. (If you don't get enough water out of your coconut, simply make up the quantity with water.) Leave the coconut to soak for about 30 minutes.

heat the vegetable oil in a large, heavy saucepan and add the onion, green pepper, and garlic. Fry gently over a very low heat, stirring occasionally, until the onion and pepper are softened and golden brown.

add the fresh root ginger, turmeric, chili peppers, cloves, and chili flakes to the onion and pepper mixture. Stir well and continue cooking over low heat for 2–3 minutes, stirring.

add the pumpkin, tomatoes, coconut, and coconut water. Bring to a boil and then reduce the heat to a bare simmer. Cover the pan and cook gently for 20 minutes, until the pumpkin is tender but not mushy. Season to taste with salt and pepper and serve hot.

Serves 6
Preparation time: *20 minutes, plus soaking*
Cooking time: *30–35 minutes*

protein 2 g • fat 5 g • cholest. 8 g

clipboard: Cloves are the immature flower buds of an evergreen tree from southeast Asia, east Africa and the West Indies. They can be bought either whole or ground, but it is better to buy them whole as ground spices soon lose their aroma.

Caponata

This Sicilian dish is often served as a cold antipasto. Pine nuts would be a tasty addition but will increase the fat content.

3 eggplant cut into ½-inch dice

2 tablespoons olive oil

I onion, thinly sliced

2 celery sticks, diced

⅓ cup strained tomato pulp (passata)

3 tablespoons wine vinegar

I yellow bell pepper, cored, seeded, and finely sliced

I red pepper, cored, seeded, and finely sliced

2 tablespoons anchovy fillets, soaked in warm water, drained and dried

2 tablespoons capers, roughly chopped

2 tablespoons pitted sliced black olives

2 tablespoons pitted sliced green olives

2 tablespoons pine nuts (optional)

salt

2 tablespoons minced parsley, to serve

put the diced eggplant into a colander, sprinkle with salt, and leave to drain on a slanted board for 15–20 minutes to remove the bitter juices. Rinse under cold running water to remove any salt and pat dry with paper towels.

heat the oil in a saucepan, add the onion and sauté until soft and golden. Add the celery and cook for 2–3 minutes. Add the eggplant and cook gently for 3 minutes, stirring occasionally. Add the passata and cook gently until it has been absorbed. Spoon in the wine vinegar and cook for 1 minute. Add the peppers, anchovies, capers, olives, and pine nuts, if desired, and cook for a further 3 minutes.

transfer the mixture to an ovenproof dish and bake, covered, in a preheated oven at 350°F for about 1 hour. Serve lukewarm or cold sprinkled with chopped parsley.

Serves 6
Preparation time: *40 minutes, plus 15–20 minutes draining time*
Cooking time: *1¼ hours*
Oven temperature: *350°F*

protein 3 g • fat 4 g • cholest. 7 g

clipboard: Passata is a convenient way of using sieved tomato pulp and is widely available in bottles and cartons from supermarkets and health food shops.

Spicy Roast Vegetables

These lightly spiced roast vegetables are delicious as an appetizer or a side-dish. Although they are called roast vegetables, they are actually better cooked in a large heavy-based broiler pan.

2 tablespoons good-quality extra virgin olive oil
½ teaspoon white cumin seeds
1 green bell pepper, cored, seeded, and thickly sliced
1 red bell pepper, cored, seeded, and thickly sliced
1 orange bell pepper, cored, seeded, and thickly sliced
2 zucchini, diagonally sliced
2 tomatoes, halved
2 red onions, quartered
1 eggplant, thickly sliced
2 thick fresh green chili peppers, sliced
4 garlic cloves
1 x 1-inch piece fresh root ginger, shredded
1 teaspoon dried crushed red chili peppers
½ teaspoon salt
1 tablespoon chopped fresh coriander, to garnish
lemon wedges, to serve

heat the broiler pan for 2 minutes. Pour in the olive oil, then add the cumin seeds. Lower the heat to medium.

arrange the vegetables in the pan with a pair of tongs, then add the green chili peppers, garlic, ginger, red chili peppers, and salt, and increase the heat. Cook the vegetables for 7–10 minutes, turning them with the tongs.

serve hot with lemon wedges and garnish with the fresh coriander.

Serves 6
Preparation time: *10 minutes*
Cooking time: *15 minutes*

protein 2 g • fat 4 g • cholest. 8 g

Two-Bean Vegetable Goulash

½ cup each black-eyed peas and Great Northern beans, soaked overnight

1 tablespoon vegetable oil

½ cup pearl onions, or shallots, peeled but left whole

4 sticks of celery, sliced into chunks

4 small zucchini, cut in chunks

3 small carrots, cut in chunks

1¼ cups canned tomatoes

1¼ cups Vegetable Broth (see page 244)

1 tablespoon paprika

½ teaspoon caraway seeds

1 tablespoon cornstarch

2 tablespoons water

salt and freshly ground black pepper

sour cream, fromage frais or low-fat crème fraîche, to serve (optional)

drain the beans and rinse under cold running water. Put them in two separate pans, cover with water, and bring to a boil. Boil fast for 10 minutes, then lower the heat, half-cover the pans, and simmer for about 1 hour until tender. Drain, rinse, and set aside.

heat the oil in a large skillet, and fry the onions, celery, zucchini, and carrots quickly over a high heat until lightly browned. Add the tomatoes with their juice and the broth. Stir in the paprika, caraway seeds, salt, and pepper, to taste. Cover and simmer for 20 minutes, until the vegetables are tender.

stir both lots of cooked beans into the vegetables. Blend the cornstarch with the water and add to the pan. Bring to a boil, stirring, until the sauce thickens a little. Cover the pan and simmer again for about 10 minutes. Spoon the goulash into a warmed dish and serve with a little sour cream, fromage frais, or low-fat crème fraîche, if desired.

Serves 4
Preparation time: *30 minutes, plus soaking*
Cooking time: *1 hour 20 minutes*

protein 13 g • fat 4 g • cholest. 41 g

clipboard: If you have neither the time nor the inclination to cook dried beans, you can always use canned beans instead.

Noodles with Vegetables

8 ounces low-fat dried egg noodles

2 tablespoons peanut oil

1 small leek, sliced

2 oyster mushrooms, torn

1 celery stick and leaf, chopped

½ cup Chinese (Napa) cabbage leaves, sliced

4 cauliflower flowerets

2 tablespoons soy sauce

1½ tablespoons sugar

½ teaspoon salt

1 teaspoon freshly ground black pepper

2 tablespoons crispy garlic

fresh coriander (cilantro), to garnish

cook the noodles in boiling water for 5–6 minutes. Drain and rinse in cold water to stop further cooking.

heat the oil in a wok or large skillet over a moderate heat, then add all of the ingredients one by one, including the noodles. Give a quick stir after each addition.

stir-fry for 3–4 minutes, adding a little more oil if necessary. Check the seasoning.

serve at once, garnished with fresh coriander (cilantro).

Serves 4
Preparation time: *10 minutes*
Cooking time: *13–15 minutes*

protein 10 g • fat 4 g • cholest. 58 g

clipboard: To make crispy fried garlic, heat about 1¼ cups peanut oil in a wok and, when the oil is hot, throw in about 6 cloves of minced garlic; stir for about 40 seconds. Remove with a slotted spoon and drain as much of the oil as possible, then spread the garlic out to dry on paper towels. You can store crispy garlic in an airtight container, where it will keep for up to 1 month. If oyster mushrooms are not available, use canned Chinese mushrooms, or fresh mushrooms.

Fish
Dishes

Plaice with Lemon Sauce

8 small plaice fillets, skinned
finely grated rind of ½ lemon
1 tablespoon minced parsley
1¼ cups skim milk
salt and freshly ground black pepper
dill sprigs, to garnish

Sauce

2 zucchini
1¼ cups Chicken Broth (see page 244)
grated rind of ½ lemon
1 garlic clove, peeled and minced

spread out the plaice fillets, skinned sides face up. Sprinkle with salt and pepper to taste, lemon rind, and parsley, and roll each one up.

for the sauce, chop the zucchini and cook together with the broth, lemon rind, and garlic until just tender.

blend the sauce ingredients in a blender until smooth.

put the rolled plaice fillets into a shallow saucepan. Add the milk and salt and pepper to taste. Cover tightly and poach the fish gently for about 8–10 minutes until it is just tender, then drain, reserving the liquid. Arrange on a warmed serving platter.

heat the sauce in a pan with just enough of the fish cooking liquid to make a fairly thick liquid.

spoon the prepared zucchini and lemon sauce around the rolled fish fillets and garnish with dill. Serve with thinly sliced zucchini.

Serves 4
Preparation time: *25–30 minutes*
Cooking time: *about 15 minutes*

protein 28 g • fat 4 g • cholest. 8 g

Monkfish Kabobs

Let your guests cook their own kabobs which you have prepared in advance. In this way, you will not still be slaving over the hot coals while everyone else is enjoying their meal. Remember to light the barbecue well ahead of time.

4 pounds monkfish, cut into 1½ inch cubes

1 teaspoon salt

4 tablespoons white wine

2 tablespoons lemon juice

1 sprig fresh rosemary, leaves chopped

1 garlic clove, crushed

3 lemons, cut into small chunks

4 green bell peppers, cored, seeded and cut into small rectangles

5 pita pockets, halved and warmed, to serve (optional)

sprinkle the monkfish with salt and pour the wine and lemon juice over it. Stir in the rosemary and garlic. Cover and marinate for 1 hour.

thread cubes of fish, chunks of lemon, and bell pepper pieces alternately onto 10 skewers. Lay the skewers on a dish, sprinkle with some of the marinade, and cover with aluminum foil.

when the charcoal is ready for cooking, place the skewers on the barbecue rack and cook for 10 minutes, turning frequently.

serve the kabobs in pockets of warm pita bread, if desired.

Serves 10
Preparation time: *10 minutes, plus marinating*
Cooking time: *10 minutes*

protein 35 g • fat 1 g • cholest. 19 g

Fish Kabobs Madras

These kabobs are made with monkfish, which holds its shape well and will not fall apart.

4 tablespoons plain low-fat yogurt

3 tablespoons lime juice

1 garlic clove, crushed

1 teaspoon curry powder

6 drops Tabasco sauce

1 thin slice fresh ginger, minced

1 pound monkfish or other firm white fish, cut into 1-inch cubes

12 jumbo shrimp

12 shelled mussels

salt and freshly ground black pepper

Garnish

1 tablespoon chopped fresh coriander (cilantro)

lime wedges

mix the yogurt with the lime juice, garlic, curry powder, Tabasco, chopped ginger, and salt and pepper, to taste.

stir the fish, shrimp, and mussels lightly into the spiced yogurt mixture; cover and chill for 4 hours.

thread the pieces of fish, shrimp, and mussels alternately on to 4 kabob skewers. Brush off any excess yogurt mixture.

place the kabobs on a lightly greased cookie sheet under a preheated broiler. Broil for about 6 minutes, or until the fish is just tender, brushing with extra yogurt marinade.

arrange the kabobs on a platter, sprinkle with coriander (cilantro), and serve with wedges of lime.

Serves 4
Preparation time: *15 minutes, plus chilling*
Cooking time: *about 6 minutes*

protein 31 g • fat 2 g • cholest. 4 g

Cod Niçoise

This colorful fish dish, with tomatoes, bell peppers, and black olives, brings a flavor of the sunny Mediterranean to your cuisine.

4 cod fillets
⅔ cup dry white wine
⅔ cup water
slice of onion
bouquet garni
1 garlic clove, crushed
2 tablespoons low-fat spread
2 tablespoons all-purpose flour
⅔ cup skim milk
2 large tomatoes, skinned, seeded, and diced
1 green bell pepper, cored, seeded and finely chopped
salt and freshly ground black pepper

Garnish
12 black olives, pitted
parsley sprigs

heat the oven to 350°F. Rinse and dry the cod, lay it in an ovenproof dish, and add salt and pepper to taste. Pour over the wine and water, adding the onion, bouquet garni, and garlic. Cover with oiled parchment paper and poach in the preheated oven for 20 minutes. Drain and reserve the liquid. Keep the fish hot.

melt the low-fat spread, stir in the flour, and cook for 1 minute. Remove from the heat and gradually stir in 1¼ cups of the fish cooking liquid and the milk. Return to the heat and bring to a boil, stirring, until thick and smooth. Simmer for 2–3 minutes, then taste and adjust seasoning. Add the tomatoes and pepper and reheat to boiling. Pour this over the fish. Garnish with olives and flat-leaved parsley. Serve with whole-wheat bread or rice.

Serves 4
Preparation time: *15 minutes*
Cooking time: *24 minutes*
Oven temperature: *350°F*

protein 42 g • fat 5 g • cholest. 9 g

Fish and seafood

Plaice

Shrimp

Haddock fillet

Sea bass

Shrimp

Shrimp are shellfish which are usually sold already cooked and should be bright pink or red in color. They can be bought either fresh, frozen, or canned and are delicious in hot or cold dishes, particularly when broiled.

Haddock fillet

Haddock is a sea fish of the cod family and is similarly low in fat and versatile. It is at its best between October and January. It can be bought whole or in fillets, fresh or frozen, and is also available smoked. Hake can be substituted.

Sea bass

Sea bass is a large, stripy fish with a very big head. It is not a common fish and is therefore fairly expensive. It is best between January and March, and then again between August and December. It is good baked, roasted, or broiled.

Plaice

Plaice is a flat fish with a mild flavor. It is at its best from June through December. It can be bought either whole or filleted and can be cooked in a great number of different ways. Porgy or skate can be used instead.

Sea bream

Rainbow trout

Monkfish tail

Cod fillet

Sea bream

Sea bream is a thick flat fish, with firm, delicately flavored, white flesh. It is sold either whole or in fillets and is good stuffed and baked, broiled or poached. Substitutes are red snapper and flounder.

Rainbow trout

Trout is a popular freshwater fish. Farmed trout are available all year round, while river trout, which is still more highly thought of, is available from March through September. It is an oily fish and is therefore relatively high in fat.

Monkfish tail

Monkfish, also known as angler fish, is a large, ugly-looking fish with an enormous head, and is actually a ray-like shark. It is a relatively expensive fish and is available all year round. It is an important ingredient in bouillabaisse and other fish soups, and can be fried, baked, or barbecued as kabobs. The flavor is similar to that of shellfish. Monkfish contains almost no fat.

Cod fillet

Cod is one of the most versatile and popular white fish. It has a coarse, flaky flesh and a mild flavor. Like several of the white fish, cod is especially low in fat and is therefore a good choice for anyone on a low-fat diet. It is plentiful all year round as fillets or steaks, fresh or frozen, and can also be bought smoked or salted.

Sea Bass Baked in Spinach

1 sea bass, weighing about 1½ pounds,
cleaned and gutted
2 cups spinach
2 shallots, chopped
⅔ cup dry white wine

Stuffing

4 tablespoons fresh bread crumbs
1 tablespoon low-fat spread, melted
2 tablespoons chopped fresh chervil
1 tablespoon chopped fresh tarragon
1 tablespoon chopped fresh basil
1 tablespoon lemon juice
salt and freshly ground black pepper

Garnish

3 orange slices, quartered
small sprigs of tarragon

mix together all the stuffing ingredients, season with salt and pepper to taste, and stuff the fish cavity.

put the spinach in a colander in a bowl and pour boiling water over it. Drain thoroughly. Wrap the stuffed sea bass in the blanched spinach, leaving the head and tail exposed. Sprinkle the shallots over the base of a gratin dish and place the fish on top. Pour the wine over it. Cover with aluminum foil and cook in a preheated oven at 400°F for 30 minutes.

transfer to a warmed serving dish and garnish with quartered orange slices and little sprigs of tarragon.

Serves 6
Preparation time: *30 minutes*
Cooking time: *30 minutes*
Oven temperature: *400°F*

protein 27 g • fat 5 g • cholest. 7 g

clipboard: Several varieties of sea-bass are available in the United States, including black bass and striped bass. Grouper, which belongs to the same family, can also be used for this dish. Here, as in other fish dishes, if the fish named in the recipe is not available, ask at the fish market for the most suitable substitute.

Sweet-and-Sour Cod Cutlets

4 individual cod cutlets or steaks
1 tablespoon sunflower margarine
1 onion, thinly sliced
⅔ cup Fish or Vegetable Broth
(see pages 244–245)
⅔ cup orange juice
2 tablespoons wine vinegar
1 tablespoon soy sauce
2 teaspoons soft brown sugar
1½ tablespoons cornstarch

Garnish
julienne strips of orange rind, blanched
spring onions

place the pieces of cod in a pan large enough to hold them in a single layer. Cover with cold water and bring slowly to a boil over a moderate heat. Poach gently for about 10 minutes or until the fish is tender.

meanwhile, melt the margarine in a pan and sauté the onion for 5–7 minutes, until soft but not brown. Add the broth, orange juice, vinegar, soy sauce, and sugar to the pan and stir well to combine.

blend the cornstarch with a little water in a small bowl to make a creamy paste and add to the sauce. Bring to a boil, stirring, until the sauce is thickened. Simmer for 3–5 minutes.

when the fish is cooked, lift the cod portions out of the pan with a slotted spoon and place in a serving dish. Pour the sauce over the fish. To serve, garnish with strips of orange rind and green onions (scallions).

Serves 4
Preparation time: *15 minutes*
Cooking time: *10 minutes*

protein 36 g • fat 5 g • cholest. 18 g

clipboard: Use any other white fish that you have available such as red snapper or porgy, fresh or frozen. If you like, fine strips of green, red, or yellow bell pepper can be added to the sauce. Serve with puréed potatoes and a seasonal green vegetable.

Portuguese Cod

Cook cod fillets in the Portuguese style to make them more interesting.

2 tablespoons low-fat spread
I onion, minced
I garlic clove, crushed
4 tomatoes, skinned and chopped
juice of I lemon
4 cod fillets
salt and freshly ground black pepper
chopped parsley, to garnish

heat the low-fat spread and soften the chopped onion over medium heat, without allowing it to brown. Add the crushed garlic, chopped tomatoes, and lemon juice. Season to taste with salt and pepper and stir well.

spoon about one-third of this sauce into a shallow ovenproof dish. Arrange the cod fillets on top, then pour the remaining sauce over them. Cover the dish with a lid or with aluminum foil and bake in a moderately hot oven at 375°F for 25–30 minutes.

remove from the oven and sprinkle with a little chopped parsley to garnish before serving.

Serves 4
Preparation time: *15 minutes*
Cooking time: *30–35 minutes*
Oven temperature: *375°F*

protein 36 g • fat 4 g • cholest. 4 g

clipboard: Cod is particularly low in fat. It has a moist, firm, creamy-white flesh, which flakes when cooked. It is extremely versatile and can be prepared in many different ways. However, prolonged cooking harms both the flavor and the presentation.

Fillet of Sole
with Melon and Mint

4 sole fillets, halved

2 tablespoons chopped mint

1¼ cups dry white wine

1 cantaloupe melon, halved and seeded

⅔ cup plain low-fat yogurt

salt and freshly ground black pepper

sprigs of fresh mint, to garnish

season the sole fillets with salt and pepper and sprinkle with half of the mint. Roll up each fish fillet and secure with wooden cocktail sticks. Place the fish rolls in a deep skillet and sprinkle over the remaining mint. Add the white wine. Cover the pan and poach gently for about 8 minutes, until the fish is tender.

meanwhile, using a melon baller, scoop the melon flesh into small balls. Cut out any remaining melon flesh attached to the skin.

carefully drain the rolled fillets, place on a warm serving platter, and keep warm. Remove the cocktail sticks.

boil the poaching liquid with the remnants of melon flesh until well reduced and whisk until smooth. If necessary, purée in a food processor or blender.

stir in the yogurt and heat the sauce through gently. Season with salt and pepper and spoon over the cooked fish. Garnish with the melon balls and sprigs of mint.

Serves 4
Preparation time: *20 minutes*
Cooking time: *10–12 minutes*

protein 29 g • fat 3 g • cholest. 12 g

Tarragon-infused Sea Bass

4 sea bass fillets
large bunch of tarragon
1 teaspoon olive oil
juice of 1 lemon
sea salt flakes and freshly ground black pepper
lemon wedges, to serve

heat the broiler and arrange the sea-bass, skin side downward, under the broiler. Cook for 3 minutes. Place a quarter of the tarragon on each fillet, pressing it into the fish.

turn the fish so that it is resting on the tarragon and cook for a further 3 minutes.

drizzle with the olive oil and lemon juice, and season. Serve with the charred tarragon and lemon wedges.

Serves 4
Preparation time: 5 *minutes*
Cooking time: 6 *minutes*

protein 34 g • fat 5 g • cholest. 1 g

Fish Pie

This is a wholesome and popular family dish. Serve it with green peas or a salad, either of which would add a touch of color.

1½ pounds cod or haddock fillets, or a mixture of white-fleshed fish

about 1¼ cups skim milk

1 bayleaf

½ onion, sliced

6 peppercorns

2 tablespoons butter or margarine

3 tablespoons all-purpose flour

2 tablespoons chopped fresh parsley or dill

4 tomatoes, skinned and sliced

2 pounds potatoes

⅔ cup hot skimmed milk

salt and freshly ground white pepper

simmer the fish gently in skim milk and water to cover, with the bayleaf, onion, and peppercorns, until cooked. Measure out the fish cooking liquid and make it up to 2 cups with more skimmed milk if necessary.

melt the butter or margarine and stir in the flour. Cook over a gentle heat for 1 minute, then stir in the strained fish cooking liquid. Bring to a boil, stirring, until the sauce is smooth and thick. Season to taste and stir in the chopped parsley or dill. Pour a little sauce into a greased ovenproof dish and lay the fish on top of it. Top with the tomato slices and cover with the remaining sauce.

meanwhile, cook the potatoes and beat to a purée with the hot skim milk. Season and pile on top of the fish mixture. Brown under the broiler for a few minutes before serving, if desired.

Serves 6
Preparation time: *10 minutes*
Cooking time: *15 minutes*

protein 27 g • fat 5 g • cholest. 46 g

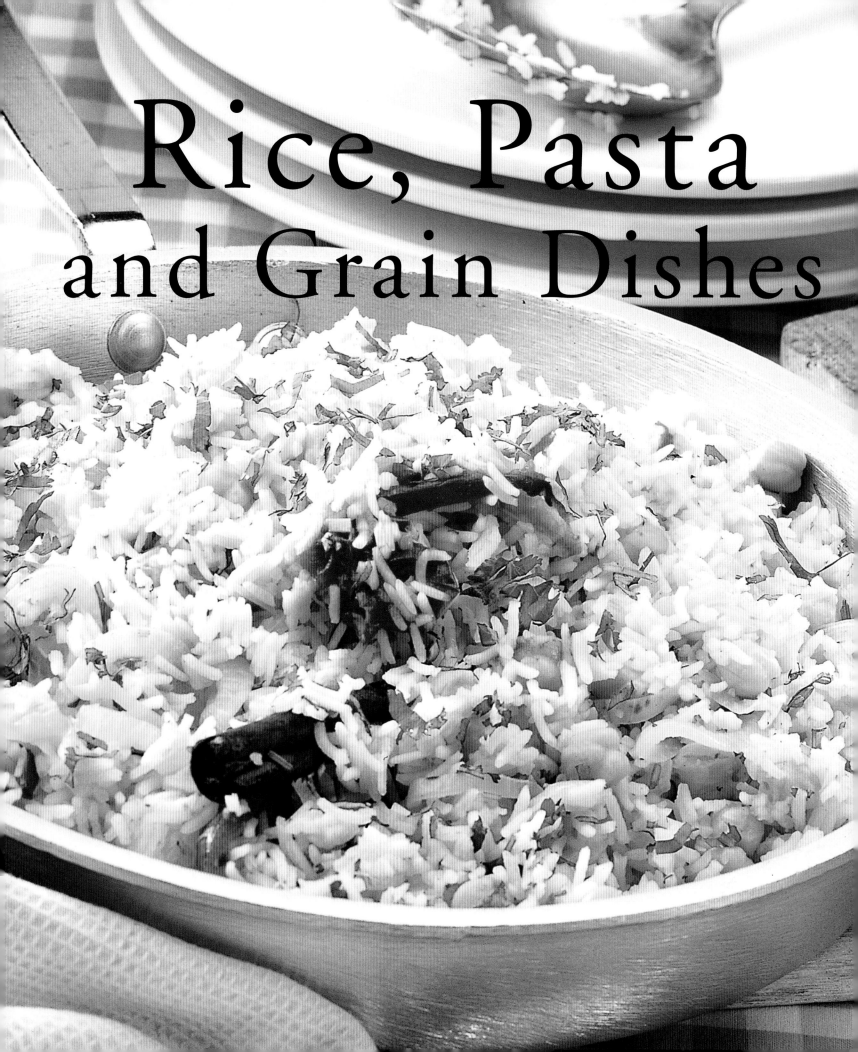

Rice, Pasta
and Grain Dishes

Rice Pilaf

One of the simplest ways of cooking rice, this is probably also one of the most delicious.

1 cup long-grain rice
1 onion, chopped
a little Chicken or Vegetable Broth (see page 244)
1 teaspoon ground turmeric
1 tablespoon currants
1 cup canned pineapple pieces, drained
salt

cook the rice in boiling salted water for 10 minutes or according to package instructions. Drain, and sprinkle with a little cold water in order to separate the grains. Keep warm in a covered dish.

cook the onion in a little broth and add the turmeric, currants, and pineapple pieces. Drain. Toss the rice in this mixture and serve.

Serves 4
Preparation time: *15 minutes*
Cooking time: *20 minutes*

protein 5 g • fat 5 g • cholest. 58 g

clipboard: Turmeric comes from the same family as ginger, and in the East it is often used fresh like ginger. It has bright orange flesh which turns yellow when dried. It is also available dried, either whole or ground, and is probably best bought ground because it is so hard, but should be bought often and in small quantities as it soon begins to taste stale. It is often used as an inexpensive alternative to saffron. Turmeric is also used as a dye, most famously in the yellow robes of Buddhist monks, so be careful when using it in the kitchen as it can stain clothes and work surfaces.

Mussel Risotto

4 cups mussels in their shells
1 teaspoon oil
1 small onion, roughly chopped
1 garlic clove, roughly chopped
⅔ cup Fish Broth (see page 245)
or white wine
grated low-fat or reduced-fat cheese, to serve
(optional)

Risotto:

1 tablespoon olive oil
2 small onions, minced
1–2 garlic cloves, minced
1½ cups arborio or Carolina rice
1 quart Fish Broth (see page 245)
salt and freshly ground black pepper

wash the mussels in plenty of cold water, discarding any that do not close when tapped sharply. Heat the oil in a large pan, add the onion and garlic, and cook for several minutes. Add the fish broth or white wine and the mussels. Heat briskly until the mussels open. Strain and reserve the cooking liquid, and remove the fish from both their shells. Do not try to force open any mussels whose shells do not open properly – simply discard them.

make the risotto: heat the oil and cook the onions and garlic gently for 5 minutes. Add the rice and stir over a low heat. Meanwhile, heat the fish broth. Add the reserved liquid from opening the mussels, plus enough hot fish broth to cover the rice. Cook steadily until the rice has absorbed the liquid, then add a little seasoning and spoon over more of the broth. Continue adding liquid until the rice is almost tender, then gently stir in the shelled mussels, reserving a few in their shells to garnish, and enough of the hot broth to produce the correct texture. Adjust the seasoning and heat for the last few minutes. Serve with a sprinkling of grated low-fat or reduced-fat cheese, if desired.

Serves 4
Preparation time: *30 minutes*
Cooking time: *20 minutes*

protein 20 g • fat 5 g • cholest. 73 g

clipboard: A risotto should have a soft, creamy texture, which is achieved by using the right kind of rice and adding the liquid gradually during the cooking process. Instead of arborio or Carolina rice, you can use short-grain — the type that is used to make milk puddings. To enjoy a risotto at its best, it should be served immediately after cooking.

Yellow Rice with Mushrooms

1 tablespoon peanut oil

2 cups cold cooked rice

½ cup snowpeas, topped and tailed

½ cup button mushrooms, halved

½ cup bamboo shoots

1 teaspoon turmeric

2 teaspoons sugar

1 tablespoon soy sauce

1 teaspoon salt

ground black pepper, to taste

Garnish

1 tablespoon crispy fried garlic (see clipboard)

1 large fresh red chili, seeded and cut into strips

heat the oil in a wok. Add the rice and give it a good stir, then add the rest of the ingredients. Stir-fry over a low heat until thoroughly mixed. Increase the heat and stir for 1–2 minutes, making sure that the rice does not stick to the wok.

turn on to a serving dish, garnish with the crispy garlic and chili and serve at once.

Serves 4
Preparation time: *3 minutes*
Cooking time: *3–4 minutes*

protein 6 g • fat 4 g • cholest. 42 g

clipboard: Bamboo shoots are part of the bamboo plant, which grows all over tropical Asia. The shoots have been used in Chinese cooking for centuries. They are sweet and crunchy, and can be bought either fresh or canned, though the fresh ones are crunchier than the canned ones.

Chick Pea and Tomato Rice

This is a versatile, lightly flavored rice. Use a good-quality basmati rice, soak it for 20–30 minutes, then drain well. The lid of the saucepan must fit well to ensure perfect rice.

1 tablespoon vegetable ghee or butter

1 teaspoon corn oil

2 onions, sliced

2 black cardamoms

1 cinnamon stick

2 whole cloves

4 black peppercorns

1 teaspoon ginger purée

1 teaspoon garlic purée

1½ teaspoons salt

2 tomatoes, sliced

1¾ cups canned chick peas (garbanzo beans), drained

1¾ cups basmati rice, washed and drained

2 tablespoons chopped fresh coriander (cilantro)

3 cups water

heat the ghee or butter with the oil in a saucepan until hot.

add the onions, black cardamoms, cinnamon, cloves, and peppercorns, and stir-fry over a high heat for about 2 minutes, then add the ginger, garlic, salt, and sliced tomatoes.

stir in the drained chickpeas (garbanzo beans) and rice and lower the heat to medium. Add 1 tablespoon of the fresh coriander (cilantro).

pour in the water, cover tightly, and cook for about 15–20 minutes or until all the water has been fully absorbed.

remove from the heat and leave to stand for 3–5 minutes before serving the rice, garnished with the remaining fresh coriander (cilantro).

Serves 6
Preparation time: *15 minutes, including standing*
Cooking time: *15–20 minutes*

protein 10 g • fat 5 g • cholest. 67 g

Mushroom Risotto

Mushroom risotto is a classic Italian dish and an all-time favorite. It requires a lot of stirring, but is well worth the effort for its deliciously creamy texture.

1 tablespoon low-fat spread
1 onion, sliced
1 cup brown medium-grain rice
⅔ cups dry white wine
2½ cups boiling Vegetable or Chicken Broth (see page 244), kept simmering
2 cups mushrooms, sliced
1 tablespoon chopped basil
1 tablespoon freshly grated Parmesan cheese
salt and freshly ground black pepper

melt the low-fat spread in a saucepan, and fry the onion until golden. Stir in the rice, and cook for 5 minutes, stirring frequently.

add the wine and bring to a boil. Continue boiling until well reduced. Stir in a ladleful of the broth, the mushrooms, basil, salt, and pepper to taste. Simmer, stirring, until all the liquid has been absorbed.

continue simmering, gradually stirring in all of the broth until the liquid has been absorbed.

stir in the grated Parmesan, and serve immediately.

Serves 4
Preparation time: *30 minutes*
Cooking time: *about 20 minutes*

protein 7 g • fat 5 g • cholest. 48 g

Noodles, Rice, and Pasta

Rice noodles

Brown rice

Long-grain rice

Short-grain rice

Rice noodles

Rice noodles are made from rice flour. Dried rice noodles are as fine as string and are widely used in Oriental cooking. They may be boiled or deep-fried quickly in hot oil. Some specialist Oriental stores also sell fresh rice noodles, which are smooth, flimsy, and have a very bland flavor.

Brown rice

Brown rice has been subjected to the absolute minimum of processing. The tough husk has been removed but the outer bran has been left intact. This means that it is a lot more nutritious than polished, or white, rice. It takes rather longer to cook. It is often used in vegetarian diets.

Long-grain rice

Long-grain rice is about four to five times as long as it is wide, with tapered ends. The cooked grains are dry, separate, and fluffy. This type of rice is used in the great majority of savory rice dishes, including the boiled or steamed rice that is served with curries, pilafs, and salads.

Short-grain rice

Short-grain rice, also known as 'pudding rice', is used for risottos, or for soups, puddings, and other desserts. There are several kinds, including arborio rice which is grown in the Po Valley of Italy. It has a particularly high starch content.

Spaghetti

Radiatore

Farfalle

Penne

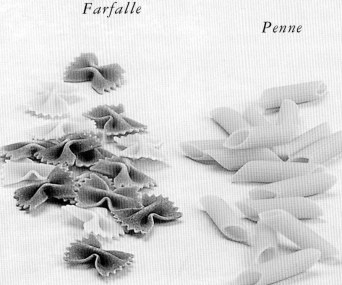

Radiatore
Pasta comes in many different shapes, and this is one of the most interesting ones available. It is shaped like little automobile radiators, hence the name. It is not as easily available as many of the more common pasta shapes. The cute shape makes it particularly popular with children.

Farfalle
Farfalle is a delightful pasta which is made in different-sized bow shapes. It is attractive served with a colorful sauce and garnished. This pasta comes in several different colors which reflect the flavoring, including red (tomato), green (spinach), white (egg), and black (cuttlefish ink).

Penne
This is a hollow, quill-like pasta, the ends of the tubes having been cut on the diagonal. It is a very versatile, popular pasta and can be bought either dried or fresh. Penne is boiled until it is just *al dente*, or firm to the bite, and served with any of the many classic pasta sauces.

Spaghetti
Spaghetti is probably the best known and most popular of all the pastas and can be bought either fresh or dried. It is also available in a low-fat form. There are a great many classic spaghetti dishes to choose from, two of the most famous ones being spaghetti bolognese and spaghetti carbonara.

Spaghetti
with Arugula & Ricotta

10 ounces spaghetti
2 teaspoons olive oil
1 small onion, minced
1 bunch of arugula, roots trimmed, leaves
finely chopped
1 garlic clove, minced
⅓ cup ricotta cheese
⅔ cups dry white wine
salt and freshly ground black pepper

plunge the spaghetti into a large saucepan of salted boiling water and simmer for 10–12 minutes or until *al dente.*

meanwhile, heat the oil, then add the onion and cook gently, stirring for 5 minutes until softened.

add the arugula, garlic, salt, and pepper to taste and stir for 2–3 minutes until the arugula has wilted. Add the ricotta and wine and stir until the ricotta has melted and is mixed evenly with the arugula.

drain the spaghetti, return to the pan and add the arugula mixture. Toss well to combine.

Serves 4
Preparation time: *10 minutes*
Cooking time: *12 minutes*

protein 12 g • fat 5 g • cholest. 59 g

clipboard: Arugula, also known as rocket plant, originates from the Mediterranean and has a pungent, slightly peppery taste. The young leaves are particularly good in salads and pasta dishes. Spinach can be used instead of arugula, but in this case you will need to be generous with the pepper.

Tagliatelle alla Siciliana

1 large eggplant, diced
1 tablespoon olive oil
2 onions, chopped
2 garlic cloves, chopped
1-13 ounce can chopped plum tomatoes
2 teaspoons chopped basil
7½ pints water
12 ounces fresh tagliatelle
salt and freshly ground black pepper
freshly grated reduced-fat Parmesan cheese,
to serve (optional)

sprinkle the diced eggplant with salt and leave to drain for 30 minutes to remove any bitter taste. Rinse in cold water and dry well with paper towels.

heat the oil in a saucepan, add the onion, garlic, and eggplant, and cook for 2–3 minutes. Add the tomatoes and their juice, together with the basil, and season to taste. Simmer for 15–20 minutes.

meanwhile, bring the water to a boil in a large pan and add salt to taste. Put in the pasta, stir, and cook for 3–4 minutes until just *al dente*.

drain the pasta, turn it into a warm serving dish and top with the eggplant mixture. Serve sprinkled with grated reduced-fat Parmesan, if desired, but remember that this will add to the fat content.

Serves 4
Preparation time: *10 minutes, plus standing*
Cooking time: *15–20 minutes*

protein 14 g • fat 5 g • cholest. 77 g

Fettuccine
with Shrimp Sauce

1 onion, chopped
2 garlic cloves, crushed
2 cups tomatoes, skinned and chopped
½ teaspoon dried basil
3 cups cooked peeled shrimp
⅔ cup white wine
2 tablespoons chopped parsley
1 pound fettucine
salt and freshly ground black pepper

put the onion and garlic into a saucepan with a little water and simmer until soft.

add the tomatoes and basil, season with salt and pepper, and simmer gently for 5 minutes. Stir in the shrimp, wine, and parsley, and simmer for a further 10 minutes.

bring a large saucepan of salted water to a boil. Add the pasta, stir and cook for 10–12 minutes until *al dente*.

drain the pasta and place on a warm serving platter. Pour the shrimp sauce over it and serve at once.

Serves 4
Preparation time: *15 minutes*
Cooking time: *about 20 minutes*

protein 37 g • fat 4 g • cholest. 98 g

Dhal

This is an unusual lentil and tomato dish, which makes a particularly good accompaniment to many rice and meat dishes. Spicy flavors are added with ginger, chilies, coriander (cilantro), cumin, and garam masala.

1 cup green lentils, soaked in cold water overnight

1 medium onion, minced

1 piece of fresh root ginger, bruised

2 bayleaves, crushed

2 fresh green chili peppers, chopped

1 tablespoon chopped fresh coriander (cilantro)

5 teaspoons olive oil

2 large garlic cloves, crushed

1 teaspoon ground coriander

½ teaspoon ground cumin

½ teaspoon garam masala

1⅓ cups tomatoes, skinned, seeded and chopped

salt

drain the lentils and put them into a pan with the onion, root ginger, bayleaves, chili peppers, fresh coriander (cilantro), 2 teaspoons of the oil, and sufficient water just to cover. Bring to a boil and simmer for about 45 minutes until the lentils are just tender. If the lentils become too dry, simply add a little extra liquid.

heat the remaining oil and fry the garlic for 4–5 minutes. Add the ground coriander, cumin, and garam masala and fry for 1 minute further. Add the tomatoes and salt to taste, and heat through.

stir the tomato and spice mixture into the lentils. Heat through gently for about 5 minutes.

serve piping hot.

Serves 4
Preparation time: *about 10 minutes*
Cooking time: *55 minutes*

protein 15 g • fat 5 g • cholest. 32 g

clipboard: To bruise root ginger means to partially crush it with the heel of a knife or using a mortar and pestle. This releases its flavor. If you have a pressure cooker, use it to cook the lentils — they will take just 5 minutes. The addition of 1 cup cooked spinach gives the most wonderful texture to the dhal.

Couscous
with Hot Peppers

2 cups couscous
⅔ cup cold water
3¾ cups Vegetable Broth (see page 244)
2 celery sticks, chopped
2 large carrots, peeled and sliced
I medium onion, peeled and thinly sliced
small bunch of herbs (one variety, or mixed)
2 garlic cloves, peeled and crushed
2 tablespoons raisins
2 tablespoons chopped almonds
I tablespoon chopped coriander (cilantro)
4 tomatoes, skinned, seeded, and chopped
I tablespoon chili sauce
salt and freshly ground black pepper

put the couscous into a large mixing bowl; sprinkle half the cold water over it evenly, and work in the couscous with your fingertips.

put the broth, vegetables, herbs, and garlic into the base of the *couscousier* (see clipboard) and bring to a boil; put the moistened couscous into the top of the *couscousier*. Cover and steam over the broth for 30 minutes; stir the grains with your fingers once or twice during this time.

turn the couscous into a large bowl. Sprinkle with the remaining water and mix in with your fingers or a wooden spoon to separate the grains. Mix in the raisins, almonds, coriander (cilantro), tomatoes, and salt and pepper to taste, and return the couscous to the top of the *couscousier*. Cover and steam for a further 30 minutes.

stir the chili sauce into the liquid in the base of the pan and heat through.

pile the hot couscous on to a warm serving dish and spoon the hot sauce and vegetables over the top. Serve immediately.

Serves 4
Preparation time: *about 30 minutes*
Cooking time: *1 hour*

protein 6 g • fat 5 g • cholest. 44 g

clipboard: The pan used for cooking couscous is called a *couscousier*. It is a double saucepan; the bottom pan contains the sauce and/or meat, and the top pan, which has a perforated base, contains the couscous grains; it is covered with a close-fitting lid on top. If you do not have such a pan, use a saucepan with a large sieve that will fit over it.

Meats

Spicy Lamb Kabobs

7 ounces leg of lamb, cut into fine strips
4 small tomatoes, halved
1 cup button mushrooms
1 green bell pepper, cored, seeded and cut
into 1 inch squares
8 bayleaves (optional)

Marinade
⅔ cup plain low fat yogurt
juice of 1 lemon
2 teaspoons salt
1 teaspoon freshly ground black pepper
1 small onion, grated

trim all visible fat from the meat. Mix together all the marinade ingredients in a bowl. Place the meat in the marinade and leave for approximately 24 hours, turning occasionally.

reserve the marinade and thread the strips of meat on to 4 long or 8 short skewers, alternating with the tomatoes, mushrooms, bell pepper, and the bayleaves, if using.

cook under a hot broiler, turning once, for 10–15 minutes. Brush the vegetables with the marinade once or twice during cooking, to prevent them drying out. Serve with boiled rice and salad.

Serves 4
Preparation time: *30 minutes,*
 plus marinating
Cooking time: *10–15 minutes*

protein 14 g • fat 5 g • cholest. 7 g

Lamb and Vegetable Hotpot

This is a comforting sort of dish, which is ideal for one of those cold wintry evenings when hot, nourishing food is a must.

5 ounces lean cooked lamb, cut into cubes

2 leeks, sliced

½ cup cauliflower, broken into flowerets

¼ cup mushrooms, sliced

1 cup sliced carrots

1 onion, sliced

2 tomatoes, sliced

⅔ cup Vegetable Broth (see page 244)

salt and freshly ground black pepper

remove any fat from the meat. Arrange the meat and vegetables, except the tomatoes, in layers in a casserole. Sprinkle on salt and pepper to taste, then arrange the tomato slices over the top. Pour in the vegetable broth and cover.

cook in the center of a preheated moderate oven at 350°F for 45 minutes. Serve hot with lima beans, if desired.

Serves 3
Preparation time: *20 minutes*
Cooking time: *45 minutes*
Oven temperature: *350°F*

protein 18 g • fat 5 g • cholest. 7 g

Thai Beef Salad

½ small Romaine lettuce, shredded

1 stalk lemongrass, chopped very finely, or finely grated rind of ½ lemon

small bunch coriander (cilantro) leaves, torn into pieces

small bunch mint leaves, torn into pieces

1 small red onion, thinly sliced

1 garlic clove, crushed

2 green chili peppers, seeded and chopped

1 tablespoon sesame oil

2 tablespoons lemon juice

1 tablespoon soft light brown sugar

12 ounces lean beef round or tenderloin, cut into fine strips

arrange a bed of lettuce leaves on 6 individual plates. Mix together the lemongrass or lemon rind, coriander (cilantro), mint, and onion, and scatter them over the lettuce. To make the dressing, combine the garlic, chili peppers, half the sesame oil, the lemon juice, and sugar.

in a large skillet or wok, heat the remaining oil and stir-fry the beef strips briskly for about 3 minutes, until lightly colored. Toss the beef strips in the dressing, spoon it quickly over the salads and serve at once.

Serves 6
Preparation time: *20 minutes*
Cooking time: *3 minutes*

protein 13 g • fat 5 g • cholest. 3 g

clipboard: Lemongrass is classified as an herb in its fresh state, but when it is dried — whether whole or in powdered form — it is regarded as a spice. It is an important flavoring in southeast Asian cuisine. When it is whole, the dried stalk should be soaked before it is used to flavor a dish, and then discarded before the dish is served. The powdered form is easier to use and does not need soaking. One teaspoon of powdered lemongrass is equivalent to one stalk of fresh lemongrass. It is more like lemon rind than lemon juice, and if you can't get a hold of it you can use lemon peel instead.

Stir-Fried Beef
with Peppers

1 tablespoon olive oil
1 onion, finely sliced
1 large garlic clove, cut into thin strips
1 pound round steak, cut into thin strips
1 red bell pepper, cored, seeded and cut into
matchstick strips
1 green bell pepper, cored, seeded and cut into
matchstick strips
1 tablespoon soy sauce
2 tablespoons dry sherry
1 tablespoon chopped fresh rosemary
salt and freshly ground black pepper
rice, to serve (optional)

heat the olive oil in a wok or deep skillet and stir-fry the onion and garlic for 2 minutes.

add the strips of beef and stir-fry briskly until evenly browned on all sides and almost tender.

add the strips of pepper and stir-fry for a further 2 minutes.

add the soy sauce, sherry, salt, and pepper to taste and the rosemary, and stir-fry for a further 1–2 minutes. Serve hot with rice, if desired.

Serves 6
Preparation time: *5 minutes*
Cooking time: *10–12 minutes*

protein 16 g • fat 5 g • cholest. 3 g

clipboard: Soy sauce is made from soy beans, wheat, water, and salt. It is routinely used in Chinese and Japanese cooking and may be used either in marinades or in the cooking process, or as a table condiment.

Italian Veal Casserole

Round-grain rice, colored with a little saffron, goes particularly well with this truly delicious and filling dish.

1 tablespoon low-fat spread
1½ pounds boned shoulder of veal, trimmed
seasoned all-purpose flour, to dust
⅔ cup dry white wine
1 Bermuda onion, finely chopped
3 cups tomatoes, skinned and roughly chopped
1 teaspoon chopped lemon thyme
½ teaspoon dried oregano
⅔ cup Chicken Broth (see page 244)
grated rind of 1 lemon
2 garlic cloves, crushed (optional)
2 tablespoons chopped parsley
salt and freshly ground black pepper

heat the low-fat spread in a heavy-bottomed flameproof stewpan. Lightly dust the veal with seasoned flour, and cook until golden.

add the wine, onion, tomatoes, herbs, broth, salt, and pepper. Bring to simmering point, cover, and cook gently for 1½–2 hours. Remove the lid after the first hour if the sauce needs reducing.

mix the lemon rind with the garlic and parsley. Sprinkle over the casserole just before serving.

Serves 6
Preparation time: *30 minutes*
Cooking time: *1½–2 hours*

protein 25 g • fat 5 g • cholest. 5 g

Veal
with Apples and Applejack

Applejack (apple brandy) adds a deliciously rich flavor to the sauce in this dish, but if you only have brandy on hand, you can use this instead.

6 veal chops or cutlets, weighing about 6 ounces each

2 teaspoons vegetable or sunflower oil

1 small onion, finely sliced

2 baking apples, cored and sliced

2 tablespoons yellow raisins

½ cup unsweetened apple juice

¼ cup applejack

salt and freshly ground black pepper

parsley sprigs, to garnish

trim any visible fat from the veal chops or cutlets. Heat the oil in a flameproof stewpan and sauté the veal for 3–4 minutes until they are lightly browned, turning them once. Add the onion and apple and fry lightly for a another 2 minutes. Stir in the yellow raisins, apple juice, and applejack. Season with salt and pepper.

cover the casserole with a lid. Place in a preheated oven at 375°F and bake for 50 minutes, or until the veal is tender. Remove the veal from the stewpan with a slotted spoon and place them on a warmed serving platter. Using the same spoon, arrange the apples, onions, and yellow raisins on top of the veal. Garnish with parsley sprigs. Pour the cooking liquid over, or serve separately as a sauce.

Serves 6
Preparation time: *20 minutes*
Cooking time: *50 minutes*
Oven temperature: *375°F*

protein 29 g • fat 5 g • cholest. 9 g

Baked Jacket Potatoes

with Ham and Cheese

4 large baking potatoes, scrubbed

I cup cottage cheese

2 tablespoons chopped chives

5 slices lean cooked ham, trimmed of
fat and diced

chili powder (optional)

freshly ground black pepper

2 tomatoes, quartered, lettuce and
green onions (scallions), to serve

prick the potatoes with a fork and wrap each one in a double thickness of foil. Place them in the coals at the edge of the barbecue, or in a preheated oven at 400°F, and cook for about 45–60 minutes, turning them over occasionally.

while they are cooking, mix together the cheese, chives, and ham, salt and pepper. Open up the foil, cut a cross in the top of each potato and pinch the sides to open them. Spoon in the filling and sprinkle with a little chili powder, if desired. Serve with the tomato quarters, lettuce, and green onions (scallions).

Serves 4
Preparation time: *15 minutes*
Cooking time: *45 minutes*
Oven temperature: *400°F*

protein 20 g • fat 5 g • cholest. 36 g

clipboard: To microwave the potatoes, prick them and place in a ring on a double layer of paper towels. Cook on high power for 16–20 minutes, turning over once. Leave to stand for 5 minutes, then split and fill as above.

Chicken,
Turkey, and Game

Andalusian Chicken

1 x 3½ pounds roasting chicken
1 teaspoon dried mixed herbs
1 cup water
1 cup chopped Bermuda onions
6 green bell peppers, cored, seeded, and diced
4 tomatoes, peeled, skinned, and roughly chopped
2 garlic cloves, crushed
1 teaspoon vegetable oil
1 cup cooked peas
1½ cups long-grain rice
pinch of saffron powder
bayleaf
salt and freshly ground black pepper

Garnish
lemon slices
chopped parsley

sprinkle the chicken with salt, pepper and herbs, and stand it in a roasting pan. Pour a cup of water round the chicken. Cover loosely with greased parchment paper or aluminum foil and roast in a moderately hot oven at 400°F for 1½ hours. Cool the chicken slightly, discard the skin, then strip the flesh from the bones and cut it into bite-sized pieces. Set aside. Use the chicken carcass and giblets to make chicken broth (see page 244), in which to cook the rice.

gently fry the onions, peppers, tomatoes, and garlic in the oil until soft and golden. Stir in the cooked, drained peas.

cook the rice in 5¾ cups chicken broth, with the saffron and bayleaf, for about 10 minutes, until tender. Drain if necessary (the rice should be quite dry) and remove the bayleaf.

now fold the chicken and rice into the onion and pepper mixture. Pile into a large, heated serving dish and garnish with the lemon slices. Serve sprinkled with parsley.

Serves 8
Preparation time: *30 minutes*
Cooking time: *1½ hours*
Oven temperature: *400°F*

protein 24 g • fat 5 g • cholest. 45 g

Lemon Chicken

1 tablespoon olive oil

1 small onion, finely sliced

4 chicken breasts, skinned and boned

2 tablespoons chopped parsley

1¼ cups Chicken Broth (see page 244)

1 tablespoon clear honey

juice of 1 lemon

2 teaspoons cornstarch

1 tablespoon water

rind of 1 lemon, cut into matchstick strips

salt and freshly ground black pepper

heat the oil in a large skillet. Add the onions and fry gently for 3–4 minutes. Add the chicken breasts and fry until lightly browned all over.

add the parsley, broth, honey, salt, and pepper to taste and lemon juice. Cover the pan and simmer gently for 20 minutes.

using a slotted spoon, remove the chicken breasts to a warmed serving dish, and keep warm.

blend the cornstarch and water to a smooth paste, stir in the hot cooking liquid, and then return to the pan. Stir over gentle heat until the sauce thickens. Add the strips of lemon rind to the sauce and spoon evenly over the chicken.

Serves 4
Preparation time: *15 minutes*
Cooking time: *30–35 minutes*

protein 17 g • fat 5 g • cholest. 9 g

clipboard: Honey is more commonly known for its use in sweet dishes but it also has a place in many meat dishes such as this, and is a popular flavoring in savory cooking around the world, including North Africa, China, and the United States.

Stir-Fried Chicken
with Crunchy Vegetables

1 teaspoon vegetable oil
1 pound chicken breasts, skinned, boned and cut into thin strips across the grain
½ cup white cabbage, shredded finely
½ cup beansprouts
1 large green bell pepper, cored, seeded and cut lengthwise into thin strips
2 medium carrots, cut lengthwise into thin strips
2 garlic cloves, crushed
freshly ground black pepper

Sauce
2 teaspoons cornstarch
4 tablespoons water
3 tablespoons soy sauce

prepare the sauce: mix the cornstarch to a thin paste with the water, then stir in the soy sauce. Set aside.

heat a wok until hot. Add the oil and heat over a moderate heat. Add the chicken strips, increase the heat to high, and stir-fry for 3–4 minutes or until lightly colored on all sides.

remove the wok from the heat and transfer the chicken to a plate with a slotted spoon. Set aside.

return the wok to a moderate heat until hot. Add all the vegetables and the garlic and stir-fry for 2–3 minutes or until the green pepper is just beginning to soften.

stir the sauce to mix, then pour into the wok. Increase the heat to high and toss the ingredients until the sauce thickens and coats the vegetables. Add the chicken with its juices and toss for 1–2 minutes or until all the ingredients are combined. Add pepper to taste and serve at once.

Serves 4
Preparation time: *15 minutes*
Cooking time: *6–10 minutes*

protein 30 g• fat 5 g • cholest. 8 g

Spiced Chicken

1 teaspoon coarsely ground cinnamon
6 chicken drumsticks, skinned
2 boned and skinned chicken breasts, cut into cubes
1¼ cups plain low-fat yogurt
2 large onions, chopped
2 fresh green chili peppers, seeded and chopped
1 teaspoon cumin seeds
1 garlic clove, peeled and chopped
1 tablespoon sweet paprika
2 tablespoons Chicken Broth (see page 244)
½ teaspoon finely grated lemon rind
1 red pepper, cored, seeded, and chopped
1 tablespoon cornstarch
salt and freshly ground black pepper

rub the cinnamon into the chicken meat, combine with the yogurt, and marinate for about 30 minutes.

lightly dry-fry the onions, chili peppers, cumin, and garlic in a casserole. Stir in the paprika.

strain the chicken meat, reserving the yogurt.

add the chicken to the casserole, stir well to coat, and then add the broth, lemon rind, red pepper, and half of the reserved yogurt. Cover and simmer slowly for about 1 hour.

combine the cornstarch with the remaining yogurt and stir it into the casserole a few minutes before serving, then bring to a boil and simmer for 1–2 minutes. Season to taste.

serve with rice.

Serves 6
Preparation time: *10 minutes, plus 30 minutes marinating time*
Cooking time: *about 1¼ hours*

protein 23 g • fat 5 g • cholest. 13 g

clipboard: Chicken absorbs the flavors of spices very well, as here. Cinnamon, chili peppers and sweet paprika are used in this recipe to produce an excellent combination of tastes.

Chicken and Zucchini Bake

This is a simple supper dish, which is particularly good served with a fresh green salad.

1½ pounds zucchini, sliced diagonally

¼ cup grated reduced-fat Edam cheese

¾ cup cooked chicken, skinned and diced

½ cup diced, cooked ham

3 tomatoes, sliced

Sauce

2 tablespoons low-fat spread

2 tablespoons all-purpose flour

1¼ cups skim milk

1 tablespoon sherry (optional)

salt and freshly ground black pepper

preheat the oven to 375°F.

cook the zucchini in boiling salted water for 4–5 minutes. Drain well on paper towels and place in an ovenproof dish.

sprinkle with 2 tablespoons of the cheese. Arrange the chicken, ham, and tomatoes in layers over the top. Sprinkle with the rest of the cheese.

make the sauce: melt the low-fat spread in a small saucepan over a moderate heat. Stir in the flour and cook for 1 minute. Gradually add the milk, stirring continuously. Bring the sauce to a boil and let it cook for 2–3 minutes. Season to taste and blend in the sherry, if using. Pour the sauce over the meat, zucchini, and tomatoes. Bake in the preheated oven for 20 minutes until golden. Serve hot.

Serves 6
Preparation time: *15 minutes*
Cooking time: *20 minutes*
Oven temperature: *375°F.*

protein 18 g • fat 5 g • cholest. 9 g

Chicken en Cocotte

1-3 pounds chicken, jointed and skinned
1 teaspoon vegetable oil
1 slice lean smoked ham, diced
4 small onions, chopped
1 garlic clove, crushed
2 tablespoons brandy
6 tomatoes, skinned and chopped
3 carrots, chopped
2 celery sticks, cut into 1½inch lengths
¼ teaspoon chopped thyme
1 bayleaf
1¼ cup red wine
salt and freshly ground black pepper
chopped parsley, to garnish

season the chicken portions with salt and pepper. Heat the oil in a flameproof stewpan or saucepan and add the diced ham and chicken portions. Cook until golden, turning. Take out the meats and set aside.

fry the onions and garlic in the pan fat until softened, stirring. Return the chicken and ham to the pan. Pour on the brandy and flambé the meat. Now add the tomatoes, carrots, celery, thyme, bayleaf, and red wine. Bring to a boil, cover and simmer for about 30 minutes, until the chicken and vegetables are tender. Remove the bayleaf before serving and sprinkle with chopped parsley.

Serves 6
Preparation time: *30 minutes*
Cooking time: *30 minutes*

protein 23 g • fat 5 g • cholest. 2 g

clipboard: bayleaves are not true herbs, as the bay tree grows up to 60 feet high but, being so highly aromatic, they have always been treated as such. They are an important ingredient in the bouquet garni and are commonly used to flavor fish and meat broths, court-bouillons, and soups, pâtés, and casseroles. They may be used either fresh off the tree or dried, and require long, slow cooking in order to make the most of their flavor.

Chicken
with Mango Sauce

Chicken and mango is a truly delicious combination. Fresh peaches may be used instead.

I large ripe mango
I cup Chicken Broth (see page 244)
3 tablespoons dry white wine
juice of ½ lemon
2 chicken breasts, skinned and boned
I tablespoon low-fat spread
I teaspoon pink peppercorns
2 tablespoons plain low-fat yogurt or
Homemade Yogurt (see page 247)
salt and freshly ground black pepper

halve and pit the mango. Cut 8 thin slices from the best-looking half of the mango. Scoop all the flesh from the remaining mango.

put the mango flesh into a blender or food processor with the chicken broth, white wine, and lemon juice, and blend until smooth.

fry the chicken breasts in the low-fat spread until evenly browned on all sides. Season with salt and pepper, add the mango sauce, and simmer, covered, for about 8 minutes.

stir in the pink peppercorns and the yogurt, and heat through. Arrange on a warmed serving platter and garnish with the slices of mango.

Serves 4
Preparation time: *25 minutes*
Cooking time: *about 15 minutes*

protein 24 g • fat 5 g • cholest. 8 g

clipboard: The mango pit runs lengthwise through the fruit. To remove it, insert the tip of a small knife at one or two points to find out which way it is running. Insert a sharp knife at one end of the mango and cut through, keeping the blade of the knife as close to the pit as possible. Repeat with the other half of the mango.

Stuffed Pot-Roasted Chicken

½ cup long-grain rice
1 x 3-pound chicken, with giblets
Chicken Broth (see page 244)
2 tablespoons raisins
1 small green bell pepper, cored,
seeded and chopped
grated rind of 1 lemon
4 medium onions, quartered
2 cups baby carrots
2 cups small tomatoes, skinned and quartered
¼ teaspoon chopped rosemary
1¼ pint dry cider
lemon juice
salt and freshly ground black pepper
chopped parsley, to garnish

cook the rice in boiling salted water for 10 minutes, until tender. Drain well. Chop the chicken liver and cook for a few minutes in a little broth. Drain. Mix together the rice, chicken livers, raisins, green bell pepper, grated lemon rind, salt, and pepper. Stuff the chicken with this mixture.

grease an ovenproof dish with a lid large enough to hold the chicken comfortably. Place the onions, carrots, and tomatoes in the bottom and lay the chicken on top. Sprinkle the chicken with the rosemary and pour the cider over it.

cover the casserole and cook in a moderate oven at 350°F for 2 hours, until the chicken is tender. Remove the lid for the last 10 minutes to brown the chicken.

remove the chicken and place on a warmed serving platter. Remove the vegetables with a slotted spoon and arrange around the chicken. Strain the juices into a small pan and add a squeeze of lemon juice. Reheat and serve separately, in a jug or sauceboat. Serve the chicken with boiled potatoes tossed in the chopped parsley.

Serves 6
Preparation time: *30 minutes*
Cooking time: *2 hours 10 minutes*
Oven temperature: *350°F*

protein 25 g • fat 5 g • cholest. 35 g

Roast Chicken with Tarragon

This great way of roasting a chicken part steams and part roasts, which preserves the juices and the flavor.

1 x 3 pound roasting chicken, with giblets
chopped tarragon, fresh or dried
twist of lemon peel
cornstarch to thicken
white wine or lemon juice
salt and freshly ground black pepper
sprigs of fresh tarragon, to garnish

remove the giblets from the chicken. Sprinkle the inside of the chicken with salt, pepper, and a little tarragon, then place the twist of lemon peel inside. Scatter some more tarragon over the outside. Season lightly. Place the chicken in a roasting pan with the giblets and pour in 1¼ cups hot water. Cover the pan loosely with aluminum foil and cook in a moderately hot oven at 400°F for about 1¼ hours. Check occasionally during cooking that the liquid in the pan has not dried out, and add a little more water if it looks low.

when the chicken is ready, the leg joint should move freely and when the leg meat is pierced with a fine skewer, the juice that runs should be clear. Lift the chicken on to a warmed carving dish and remove the giblets. Pour off any fat from the juices left in the pan and thicken with a little cornstarch moistened in cold water. Add a dash of white wine or a squeeze of lemon juice and strain. Garnish with the tarragon and serve with seasoned vegetables. Do not eat the chicken skin.

Serves 6
Preparation time: *20 minutes*
Cooking time: *1 hour 15 minutes*
Oven temperature: *400°F*

protein 24 g • fat 5 g • cholest. 1 g

Broiled Deviled Chicken

Mustard, ginger, Worcestershire sauce, sugar, and lemon are used in this traditional recipe to give the chicken a bit of a kick! Serve with a green salad and rice pilaf.

4 chicken portions, skinned
1 tablespoon French mustard
1 teaspoon ground ginger
1 teaspoon salt
1 teaspoon freshly ground black pepper
1 teaspoon Worcestershire sauce
½ teaspoon sugar
juice of 1 lemon

place the chicken portions in a shallow ovenproof dish. Mix together the mustard, ginger, salt, pepper, Worcestershire sauce, sugar, and lemon juice. Use to coat the chicken portions and leave to marinate for several hours, turning occasionally in the marinade.

place the chicken portions under a preheated broiler or on a barbecue, not too close to the coals. Allow 15–20 minutes on each side, although the cooking time may be shorter if you do this on an outside barbecue.

Serves 4
Preparation time: *10 minutes, plus marinating*
Cooking time: *30–40 minutes*

protein 33 g • fat 5 g • cholest. 2 g

Traditional Roast Turkey

1 x 10-pound turkey
1 tablespoon dried basil
2½ cups Chicken or Vegetable Broth
(see page 244)
5 tablespoons port wine
1 tablespoon cornstarch
salt and freshly ground black pepper

Stuffings
4 cups chestnuts
¾ cup mashed potato
5 tablespoons fresh bread crumbs
1 heaping tablespoon yellow raisins
1 garlic clove, crushed
2 celery sticks, finely chopped
2 tablespoons chopped parsley
grated rind of 1 lemon
a little grated fresh root ginger
3 tablespoons medium-dry sherry
salt and freshly ground black pepper

prepare the stuffings for the neck and carcass in advance. Make a slit on the rounded side of the chestnuts. Drop, four at a time, into a small pan of boiling water for 3 minutes. Peel and skin. Cook the chestnuts gently in fresh boiling water for about 20 minutes. Drain, then mash with a fork. Mix a quarter of the chestnuts with the mashed potato and salt and pepper. Use to stuff the neck of the bird. Mix the remaining chestnuts with the rest of the stuffing ingredients and use to stuff the turkey carcass.

stand the bird in a large roasting pan and sprinkle with basil and salt and pepper. Pour the broth round the bird and cover the pan loosely with a piece of greased aluminum foil. Cook in a moderate oven at 350°F, allowing 15–20 minutes per pound, plus 20 minutes extra. Turn the turkey, on its side or upright, every 30 minutes, and baste frequently.

remove the foil 20 minutes before the end of the cooking time, to brown the bird, turning it breast side up. Pour off the pan juices to make gravy. Skim off all the fat and boil up the juices with the port. Moisten the cornstarch with a little cold water and stir into the gravy, to thicken. Keep warm in a sauceboat until ready to serve. Remember not to eat the turkey skin, which is the most fatty part of the bird. Serve with vegetables.

Serves 8–10
Preparation time: *45 minutes*
Cooking time: *3 hours 10 minutes–4 hours*
Oven temperature: *350°F*

per serving of 100 g/3½ oz of meat:
protein 31 g • fat 5 g • cholest. 29 g

Turkey in Vermouth

White vermouth gives an unusual and interesting flavor to this turkey recipe. The stuffing, which contains lemon rind, herbs, bread crumbs, and grapes, is another successful addition.

1 x 7–8 pound turkey
1 tablespoon chopped tarragon
1 small onion, chopped
2 celery sticks, chopped
4 carrots, chopped
1¼ cups dry white vermouth

Stuffing

6 tablespoons fresh white bread crumbs
grated rind of 1½ lemons
4 tablespoons chopped parsley
½ tablespoon chopped thyme
½ cup green grapes, halved and seeded
1 egg, beaten
salt and freshly ground black pepper

mix together the dry stuffing ingredients and bind with a little egg. Do not make the mixture too wet. Spoon the stuffing into the bird. Sprinkle the turkey with the chopped tarragon. Lay the onion, celery, and carrots in the base of a large oblong casserole dish or roasting pan. Place the turkey on the bed of vegetables and pour round the vermouth. Cover and cook in a moderately hot oven at 375°F for 2½–3 hours, or until cooked. Baste from time to time with the pan juices. Add a little hot giblet broth or water, if necessary, to keep the dish moist.

slice the turkey, which should be succulent and tender, and serve with a spoonful of stuffing and the strained juices from the casserole. Remember not to eat the turkey skin.

Serves 6
Preparation time: *20 minutes*
Cooking time: *2½–3 hours*
Oven temperature: *375°F*

protein 31 g • fat 4 g • cholest. 15 g

Turkey Burgers
with Barbecue Sauce

Serve these burgers with whole-wheat rolls and a varied selection of relishes and salads.

2 pounds lean ground turkey meat
1 onion, minced
1 tablespoon white wine
1 teaspoon chopped tarragon or parsley
salt and freshly ground black pepper

Sauce
1 tablespoon low-fat spread
1 medium onion, finely sliced
2 garlic cloves, crushed
1 green bell pepper, cored, seeded and sliced
½ cup mushrooms, sliced
1¾ cups canned chopped tomatoes
2 teaspoons dried oregano
1 teaspoon Tabasco sauce
salt and freshly ground black pepper

place the ground turkey in a large bowl and add the onion, wine, and herbs. Mix together well and season to taste. Shape into 12 burgers. Place on a baking tray and set aside.

to make the sauce, melt the low-fat spread in a skillet over a moderate heat. Cook the onion and garlic until pale golden. Add the pepper and continue cooking for 5 minutes. Add the mushrooms, tomatoes, and oregano and cook for a further 5–10 minutes. Add the Tabasco and season to taste.

heat the broiler to moderate and broil the burgers, brushing with a little sunflower oil if necessary, for about 7 minutes on each side.

serve immediately, with the sauce served separately.

Serves 6
Preparation time: *30 minutes*
Cooking time: *20–25 minutes*

protein 79 g • fat 5 g • cholest. 5 g

clipboard: Chicken may be used in place of turkey. The burgers can be cooked on a barbecue instead of under the grill.

Sweet-and-Sour Chinese Turkey

1 pound turkey breast

2 tablespoons lemon juice

5 tablespoons orange juice

4–5 celery sticks

2 persimmons

8–10 radishes

½ Chinese (Napa) cabbage

1 large green bell pepper, cored and seeded

1 tablespoon oil

⅔ cup Chicken Broth (see page 244)

1½ teaspoons cornstarch

1 tablespoon soy sauce

1 tablespoon clear honey

cut the turkey breast into thin strips. Marinate in the lemon and orange juices for 30 minutes.

cut the celery, persimmon, radishes, Chinese (Napa) cabbage, and green pepper into small pieces. Heat the oil in a large nonstick skillet or wok.

drain the turkey and reserve the marinade. Fry the turkey in the oil until nearly tender. Add the vegetables and persimmons and heat for 2–3 minutes only. Blend the chicken broth with the marinade and the cornstarch. Add the soy sauce and honey. Pour this mixture over the ingredients in the pan and stir until thickened. Serve immediately.

Serves 4
Preparation time: *15 minutes, plus marinating*
Cooking time: *15–20 minutes*

protein 29 g • fat 5 g • cholest. 11 g

clipboard: Make sure you use very ripe persimmons, when unripe their high tannic acid content makes the fruit taste "furry" in the mouth.

Turkey and Parma Ham Kabobs

1 pound lean turkey meat, cut into 1½ inch cubes
grated rind of 1 lemon
1 small onion, finely chopped
1 garlic clove, finely chopped
1 teaspoon pesto sauce
2 teaspoons oil
4 ounces Parma ham, cut into long strips
8 small button mushrooms
8 small bayleaves
wedges of lemon
salt and freshly ground pepper
shredded lettuce, to serve

put the turkey into a shallow dish. Mix the lemon rind with the onion, garlic, pesto, and oil, and season to taste with salt and pepper.

stir the marinade into the turkey, cover, and chill for 3–4 hours.

drain the turkey, reserving the marinade. Wrap each piece of turkey in a strip of Parma ham.

thread the turkey and ham rolls on to kabob skewers, alternating with the mushrooms, bayleaves, and wedges of lemon.

brush the threaded skewers with the marinade, broil for 4–5 minutes. Turn the kabob skewers, brush once again with the marinade, and broil for a further 4–5 minutes.

serve piping hot on a bed of shredded lettuce.

Serves 4
Preparation time: *20 minutes, plus marinating*
Cooking time: *10 minutes*

protein 32 g • fat 5 g • cholest. 2 g

clipboard: The ham will wrap around the turkey more easily if it is moist. It is important, therefore, to keep it closely covered in the refrigerator so that it does not dry out.

Rabbit with Rosemary *and Mustard*

I medium onion, minced
I teaspoon olive oil
4 rabbit portions
I¼ cup Chicken Broth (see page 244)
I cup dry white wine
2 teaspoons coarse-grain mustard
I tablespoon chopped rosemary
3 tablespoons low-fat fromage frais
I egg yolk
salt and freshly ground black pepper
sprigs of rosemary, to garnish

fry the onion gently in the olive oil for 3 minutes. Add the rabbit portions and brown evenly on all sides.

add the chicken broth, white wine, mustard, rosemary, salt, and pepper to taste. Cover and simmer for 45 minutes until the rabbit is just tender.

remove the rabbit portions to a serving dish and keep warm.

boil the cooking liquid rapidly until reduced by half; beat the fromage frais with the egg yolk and whisk into the cooking liquid over a gentle heat, without boiling.

spoon the sauce over the rabbit and garnish with sprigs of rosemary.

Serves 4
Preparation time: *about 10 minutes*
Cooking time: *about 55 minutes*

protein 18 g • fat 5 g • cholest. 5 g

clipboard: If you are using frozen rabbit, make sure the pieces are completely thawed before cooking. Other mustards can be used but they will not give quite the same pungency and texture as coarse-grain mustard.

Desserts

Marinated Nectarines

4 large ripe nectarines
I lemon
I large orange
I cup water
4 tablespoons dry vermouth

skin the nectarines. Peel the lemon thinly and cut into matchstick strips. Squeeze the lemon juice into a large bowl and fill up with iced water. Put the prepared nectarines into the lemon water.

peel the orange thinly, removing all the white parts; chop the flesh into pieces, discarding any seeds. Cut the orange rind into matchstick strips. Put the orange flesh into a blender with the water and vermouth, and blend until smooth.

lift the nectarines out of the lemon water and drain. Put the nectarines into a shallow dish and spoon over the prepared orange and vermouth sauce. Cover and chill for 2 hours — no longer or the nectarines are likely to discolor.

sprinkle with the strips of lemon and orange rind and serve immediately.

Serves 4
Preparation time: *25 minutes, plus chilling*

protein 2 g • fat 0 g • cholest. 17 g

clipboard: To skin a nectarine, nick the stalk end with a sharp knife and plunge the fruit into boiling water for 45 seconds. The skin will then slide off easily.

Seasonal Berries

1 cup blueberries, topped and tailed

2 cups strawberries, hulled and quartered or halved, according to size

2 cups raspberries, hulled

1 cup cultivated blackberries, topped and tailed

1 cup loganberries, hulled

1¼ cups rosé wine

½ teaspoon ground allspice

combine all the berries in a serving bowl.

heat the wine in a saucepan to boiling point, add the allspice and pour over the fruit at once.

cool and stand at room temperature for 4–6 hours before serving.

Serves 4
Preparation time: *10 minutes*
Cooking time: *5 minutes, plus standing*

protein 4 g • fat 1 g • cholest. 23 g

clipboard: Other berry fruits, such as boysenberries, can also be used.

Citrus Fruit Salad

2 limes, peeled and thinly sliced

1 small lemon, peeled and segmented

4 sweet oranges, peeled and coarsely chopped

4 mandarin oranges, peeled and coarsely chopped

2–3 grapefruit, peeled and coarsely chopped

12 kumquats (optional)

1 teaspoon granulated sugar

1 teaspoon Angostura bitters

3 tablespoons sparkling mineral water

1 bunch of fresh mint

shredded mint leaves, to garnish

using a potato peeler, take a wafer-thin sliver from the discarded skins of all the citrus fruits except the kumquats.

using a pestle and mortar, crush the slivers with the sugar to release the highly flavored oils, combine with the Angostura bitters and mineral water and set aside.

place the fruit in a deep bowl. Halve the unpeeled kumquats and add them. Strain the mineral water and stir it in.

plunge the bunch of fresh mint, tied with a piece of thread, in and out of boiling water, then straight into the fruit. Chill, covered, for 2 hours.

remove the mint before serving and stir in the shredded mint leaves.

Serves 6
Preparation time: *45–55 minutes, plus chilling*

protein 3 g • fat 0 g • cholest. 29 g

clipboard: The mixture of all these different citrus fruits — lime, lemon, orange, mandarin orange, and grapefruit is wonderful. If the fruit salad is too sharp, add 1 tablespoon honey, which you have heated slightly beforehand so that it mixes in easily.

Pears with Fresh Raspberry Sauce

The combination of pears with fresh, mouth-puckering raspberry sauce is magic.

4 large firm pears
1¼ cups orange juice
bayleaf
small piece of cinnamon stick
1 tablespoon clear honey
1 cup fresh raspberries

peel and halve the pears, then core them. Place them in a saucepan with the orange juice, bayleaf, cinnamon stick, and honey. Cover the pan and simmer gently for 10 minutes.

turn the pear halves over in their cooking liquid; cover the pan and leave them to cool in their liquid.

blend the raspberries in a blender until smooth. Add enough pear cooking liquid to give a thin coating consistency.

arrange the drained pear halves in a shallow serving dish and trickle over the prepared sauce.

Serves 4
Preparation time: *about 20 minutes, plus cooling*
Cooking time: *10 minutes*

protein 7 g • fat 2 g • cholest. 31 g

clipboard: Another way of serving these pears is to spoon the raspberry sauce onto individual serving plates. Trickle a little plain low-fat yogurt on top, and arrange the pear halves carefully on top.

Whole-wheat Fruit Pancakes

Pancakes

4 tablespoons plain whole-wheat flour

4 tablespoons all-purpose flour, sifted

1 egg, beaten

1¼ cup skim milk

sunflower oil, for frying

Filling

3 large oranges, peeled, segmented and chopped

2 cups pineapple pieces in natural juice

2 tablespoons chopped walnut

2 teaspoons arrowroot

⅔ cup pure orange juice

2 tablespoons kirsch (optional)

make the pancake mixture: place the flours in a mixing bowl and make a well in the center. Add the egg and mix in well with a wooden spoon. Pour in half the milk slowly and beat thoroughly. Add the remaining milk and stir well so that the batter has a smooth, creamy consistency.

heat a little oil in a 6 inch nonstick skillet. Pour a little pancake mixture into the pan. Tilt the pan to spread it thinly and evenly. Cook until golden brown, then turn over and cook the other side. Repeat until all the mixture has been used. Stack the pancakes on a warmed plate with rounds of nonstick baking paper between them. Keep warm.

prepare the filling: place the orange pieces in a bowl. Drain the pineapple and reserve the juice. Chop the pineapple and add it to the orange with the walnuts. Blend the arrowroot with a little of the pineapple juice until smooth. Place the arrowroot mixture, pineapple, and orange juice in a small pan. Bring to the boil over a moderate heat, stirring continuously until smooth and thickened. Add the kirsch, if using.

pour a little sauce over the fruit and nuts to coat them. Mix together. Spoon the filling down the center of the pancakes and fold into triangles. Transfer to a warmed serving dish and serve. Serve the sauce separately.

Serves 6
Preparation time: *30 minutes*
Cooking time: *30 minutes*

protein 7 g • fat 5 g • cholest. 35 g

Honeyed Apples

Nuts, dates, lemon, honey, and cinnamon – this combination is true bliss!

4 medium cooking apples, cored
1 tablespoon chopped nuts, toasted
1 tablespoon chopped dates
juice of ½ lemon
about 2 tablespoons clear honey
½ teaspoon ground cinnamon

wash the apples and peel the top half. Place in an ovenproof dish. Mix the remaining ingredients together and use to fill the centers of the apples.

pour a little more honey over the apples and cook, covered, in a moderately hot oven at 375°F for about 45 minutes.

Serves 4
Preparation time: *20 minutes*
Cooking time: *45 minutes*
Oven temperature: *375°F*

protein 2 g • fat 2 g • cholest. 27 g

Fruits

Apples

Peaches

Strawberries

Dried figs

Dried dates

Dried figs

Fig trees grow in the Mediterranean and in California, where the best-known variety was introduced by the Spanish missionaries, hence the name Mission Fig. Fresh figs do not travel particularly well and are therefore often dried or preserved. They are very sweet and make wonderful preserves and desserts.

Dried dates

Dates originate from the Middle East but most dates eaten in the U.S. are from Indio, California. Dates are an excellent source of vitamins and minerals and are very sweet so do not need added sugar. They can be used in sweet and savory dishes, and combine particularly well with black or English walnuts in breads, cakes, and cookies.

Strawberries

The strawberry was introduced from Europe and remains today one of our most highly prized summer fruits. A juicy red berry with seed-pitted skin, it is best eaten simply — either on its own, or with the addition of cream – and requires remarkably little processing in the kitchen, though it is often combined with shortcake.

Peaches

Said to be the emblem of immortality, the peach is a Chinese fruit which came to Europe with the Romans. With its velvet downy skin and its succulent white or yellow flesh, it is the perfect dessert fruit. It can be incorporated into fruit salads or used to make a variety of delicious desserts and pies. It also makes a tasty fruit juice.

Apples

The apple probably originated in southwest Asia. There are thousands of varieties, whose colors range through green, red, or yellow, with a creamy white flesh. Apples can be eaten raw, but are also stewed, baked, or used in a variety of desserts, including tarts and pies. Apples are rich in vitamins and minerals, so the old saying is no lie.

Mangoes

Limes

Apricots

Red currants

Mangoes

The mango originated in India, and Buddha himself is said to have reposed in a mango grove. A perfectly ripe mango, with its smooth skin and its sweet green, yellow, orange, or pink flesh, requires no further improvement. It is the perfect addition to fruit salads, makes a truly delicious ice cream, and no curry is complete without the addition of a spoonful or two of mango, or mango-and-lime, chutney.

Limes

The lime tree is the smallest cultivated member of the citrus family, and has the smallest fruits. Lime juice is aromatic, tasty, and refreshing,and not as sharp-tasting as lemon juice. Key limes and Persian limes are grown mainly in Florida.

Apricots

Providing that it is at just the right state of ripeness and in absolutely perfect condition, the apricot is one of the most delectable fruits that you can eat. It is in season in late spring. Said to have been brought to Europe from northern China in the 16th century, the apricot became popular in Middle Eastern cookery, largely because of its perfect compatibility with lamb. It is delicious either raw or cooked, and is suitable in both sweet and savory dishes. It can be made into wine, and is also available dried. Given its tremendous versatility, the apricot deserves a special place in every cook's repertoire.

Red currants

Red currants are the only member of this family which are cultivated in the United States (black- and whitecurrants are grown in Europe), and are not always available. Blueberries can be substituted. Red currants are rich in vitamin C and have a tart flavor. Red currant jelly is eaten as an accompaniment to certain meats, particularly game and turkey; if it is not available, use cranberry sauce or jelly.

Sliced Figs with Lemon Sauce

8 plump ripe fresh figs
2 tablespoons lemon juice
⅔ cup unsweetened apple purée
grated rind of ½ lemon
3 tablespoons plain low-fat yogurt
artificial sweetener
1 tablespoon chopped pistachio nuts
4 twists of lemon peel, to decorate (optional)

cut each fig into 4 wedges. (Alternatively, the figs can be sliced, provided they are not too soft.) Sprinkle the cut figs with lemon juice.

mix the apple purée with the lemon rind and yogurt. Add sweetener to taste and half the chopped pistachios.

spoon a pool of the lemon and pistachio sauce on to each of 4 small plates and arrange the pieces of fig decoratively on top.

sprinkle with the remaining pistachio nuts and decorate with twists of lemon peel, if desired.

Serves 4
Preparation time: *15–20 minutes*

protein 5 g • fat 4 g • cholest. 18 g

clipboard: Figs have a very short season, so look for them in the stores and grab them as soon as you can. The recipe for this dish was made in heaven!

Chocolate Soufflé

vegetable oil, for greasing
⅓ cup fresh orange juice
⅓ cup sugar
4 large egg whites
2 tablespoons unsweetened cocoa powder
2 tablespoons orange liqueur
½ cup low-fat vanilla ice cream, softened

grease 6 cups with the oil.

heat the orange juice and sugar in a small saucepan for 3–4 minutes over medium to high heat, stirring occasionally, until the mixture takes on a syrupy consistency. Remove from the heat.

beat the egg whites in a large bowl until stiff, stopping before dry peaks form. Pour the syrup over the egg whites and beat for 2 minutes. Add the cocoa powder and liqueur and beat only until well mixed. Pour into the prepared cups.

bake in a preheated oven at 300°F for 5–6 minutes or until the soufflés are puffed. Be careful not to overbake the soufflés or they will become tough. Cooking time will vary slightly depending on size of cups used.

spoon 2 tablespoons of softened vanilla ice cream into the center of each soufflé. Serve immediately.

Serves 4
Preparation time: *10 minutes*
Cooking time: 5–6 *minutes*
Oven temperature: 300°F

protein 3 g • fat 3 g • cholest. 19 g

clipboard: Slices of fresh orange or crystallized orange would both make an attractive decoration for this chocolate soufflé and would reinforce the orange liqueur.

Dairy produce

Edam

Quark

Low-fat cream cheese

Quark
This low-fat cheese which has a pleasantly creamy texture, originates from Germany and Austria, and has recently become available in the United States . White in color with a smooth spreadable texture, it is similar to cottage cheese. It can be used in many sweet and savory dishes.

Edam
Edam cheese is one of the best-known of the Dutch cheeses. It is made from cow's milk and has a slow fermentation period. It is a softish cheese, free from holes, and is covered in red wax. It is fairly low in fat and reduced-fat versions, which are still lower in fat, are also available.

Low-fat cream cheese
A soft white, smooth-textured cheese made from milk and cream, cream cheese is delicious with bread or incorporated into a dressing for potatoes and salads. The low-fat variety has had its fat content reduced and is therefore the best choice when you are following a low-fat diet.

Skimmed milk

Low-fat yogurt

Virtually fat-free fromage frais

Low-fat crème fraîche

Skimmed milk
In order to be labeled as skim milk, the milk must have as little fat as possible, until the fat content is less than 0.5 percent. Skim milk contains just as much calcium as whole milk and is therefore just as nutritious.

Low-fat yogurt
Yogurt is of great benefit to the digestive system. It can be either plain or fruit-flavored. It is also available in low-fat or non-fat versions and is used in many sweet and savory dishes, especially in Middle Eastern cuisine.

Virtually fat-free fromage frais
Fromage frais is a low-fat soft white cheese, originally from France. Its consistency depends very much on its fat content, and a virtually fat-free version is now available. It can be eaten by itself or used in cooking, or served as an accompaniment instead of cream.

Low-fat crème fraîche
Crème fraîche is cream to which a lactic acid bacteria culture has been added. This has the effect of thickening the cream, as well as giving it a distinctive sharp flavor. It can be used in many sweet and savory dishes, and is a good substitute for sour cream. Low-fat crème fraîche has had some of the fat skimmed off and is therefore much lower in fat than full-fat crème fraîche.

Apricot Cheesecake

1¾ cup canned apricot halves in natural juice

2 packets orange gelatin

1 cup low-fat quark

⅔ cup plain low-fat yogurt

apricot jam, warmed and sieved, to garnish

1 tablespoon flaked almond, toasted (optional)

Cookie base

4 graham crackers

4 tablespoons low-fat spread

line the base of an 7 inch shallow cake pan with nonstick baking paper. Strain the juice from the apricots into a bowl. Make up to ⅔ cup with water, if necessary. Pour the liquid into a small saucepan and bring to a boil. Add the gelatin and stir until dissolved. Return the gelatin to the jug and leave to cool.

choose 10 apricot halves for decoration and set aside. Purée the remaining apricots with the quark and yogurt in a blender or push them through a sieve. Stir in the cooled jelly.

pour the mixture into the cake pan and place in the refrigerator for 2–3 hours to set lightly.

crush the graham crackers. Melt the low-fat spread in a pan and stir in the crumbs. Spread this over the cheese base evenly, pressing it down gently. Leave the cheesecake in the fridge for about 6–8 hours until set.

dip the pan into warm water for a few seconds to loosen it before turning out the cheesecake. Invert the pan onto a flat plate and turn out the cake. Decorate with the reserved apricot halves, glaze with warmed apricot jam, and top with almonds, if desired, though these will increase the fat content.

Serves 8
Preparation time: *30 minutes, plus setting*

protein 7 g • fat 5 g • cholest. 28 g

Whole Strawberry Ice Cream

3 egg yolks

1 tablespoon redcurrant jelly

1 tablespoon red vermouth

1¼ cups plain low-fat yogurt

1½ cups ripe strawberries, hulled

4–6 strawberries with stalks, halved, to garnish

put the egg yolks into a food processor with the redcurrant jelly, vermouth, yogurt, and half the strawberries, and blend until smooth.

transfer the mixture to a shallow container, and freeze until the ice cream starts to harden around the edges.

tip the ice cream back into a bowl and beat to break up the ice crystals. Chop the remaining strawberries and mix into the semi-set ice cream. Return to the container and freeze until quite firm.

scoop the ice cream into stemmed bowls or glasses and decorate each one with strawberry halves.

Serves 4
Preparation time: *25 minutes, plus freezing*

protein 7 g • fat 5 g • cholest. 15 g

Fresh Lime Sherbet

This is a beautiful color and has an unbelievably refreshing flavor — just the thing for those hot summer days.

3 limes

¾ cup superfine sugar

2½ cups water

I egg white, stiffly beaten

pare the rinds of the limes with a potato peeler; reserve and squeeze the juice. Dissolve the sugar in the water and bring to a boil. Boil for 3 minutes. Add the lime rinds and boil hard for a further 3 minutes, uncovered. Remove the lime rinds and set aside.

cool then add the lime juice. Strain into a freezerproof plastic carton and freeze until mushy. Stir thoroughly, mixing the sides into the center, then carefully fold in the stiffly beaten egg white. Refreeze, covered, until firm.

serve in bowls, decorated with the reserved lime rinds, with small cookies, such as almond cookies or vanilla wafers.

Serves 4
Preparation time: *20 minutes, plus freezing*
Cooking time: *6 minutes*

protein 1 g • fat 0 g • cholest. 46 g

Breads

Flours, Grains, and Beans

Puy lentils

Bulgur wheat   *Buckwheat flour*   *Graham flour*

Bulgur wheat
Bulgar wheat is made from cracked whole wheat berries, including the wheatgerm, and is therefore rich in protein, mineral salts, and carbohydrates. It has a distinctive flavor and is used in many vegetarian and Middle Eastern dishes, including salads and stews.

Buckwheat flour
Buckwheat flour is made from roasted buckwheat seeds (kasha) and is used as in pancakes, blinis, crisp thin cakes, and Japanese soya noodles (soba). Buckwheat originated in central Asia and was brought to Russia, where it is used as a staple food by the Tartars.

Graham flour
Graham and whole-wheat flours containing bran are healthy options as they are rich in dietary fiber and vitamins. Freshly milled graham flour has a nutty aroma and gives a strong texture to bread. It is often used in yeastless breads, such as Irish soda bread.

Puy lentils
Lentils are small, round, dry, flat seeds. They are particularly rich in carbohydrates, protein, phosphorus, iron, and B vitamins, and are a good addition to a child's diet. They can be used in soups, casseroles, salads, or as an accompanying vegetable, Their flavor goes especially well with pork. Lentils may be green (the Puy lentil), red (the Egyptian lentil). or brown. Lentils are beans which do not need soaking before being cooked, which makes them particularly convenient to use .

Kidney beans

Red split peas

Pinto beans

Canned chick peas

Red split peas

These are small dried peas, which have been split in two. Like many pulses, they are especially rich in carbohydrates, proteins, phosphorus, and potassium, and therefore play an important part in a healthy diet. They should always be soaked before cooking, and are often used in soups and stews. They are also available canned.

Pinto beans

The pinto bean is a variety of kidney bean. It is pale in color with red markings and is a staple of the Mexican diet. It is available dried or canned.

Kidney beans

These are the seeds of the haricot bean. They are a glossy dark reddish-brown color, and are shaped like a kidney — hence the name. They are used in spicy dishes such as chili con carne and in many Mexican dishes. The beans can also be cooked and eaten cold in salads. They are available dried, in which case they must be soaked before cooking. The soaking water must be discarded and the beans must be boiled for at least 10 minutes.

Canned chick peas (garbanzo beans)

Chick peas are the round, pea-like seeds of a leguminous plant. They are available dried, in which case they need soaking, and canned. They are rich in carbohydrate, protein, phosphorus, calcium, and iron. They are used in soups, stews, and salads and are found in Mediterranean and Mexican cooking.

Whole-wheat Soda Bread

2 cups all-purpose flour
1 teaspoon baking soda
2 teaspoons cream of tartar
2 teaspoons salt
3 cups whole-wheat flour
1¼ cups milk
4 tablespoons water
flour, to sprinkle

sift the all-purpose flour, baking soda, cream of tartar, and salt into a mixing bowl. Stir in the whole-wheat flour, then add the milk and water, and mix to a soft dough.

turn on to a floured surface, knead lightly, then shape into a large round about 2 inches thick.

place on a floured baking tray, cut a deep cross in the top of the loaf, and sprinkle with flour. Bake at 425°F for 25–30 minutes. Cool on a wire rack.

Makes 1 x 1 pound 6 ounce loaf
  (12 slices per loaf)
Preparation time: *20 minutes*
Cooking time: *25–30 minutes*
Oven temperature: *425°F*

per slice: *protein 7 g • fat 1 g • cholest. 34 g*

clipboard: To bake in a microwave oven, place on a large greased plate. Microwave on Medium (50%) power for 5 minutes, giving the plate a half turn twice. Increase the power setting to Full (100%) and microwave for a further 3 minutes, giving the plate a half-turn twice. Allow to stand for 10 minutes before transferring to a cooling rack.

Fig Loaf

This is a deliciously moist loaf, thanks to the addition of figs and molasses.

I cup bran flakes
½ cup dark soft brown sugar
½ cup chopped dried figs
2 teaspoons black-strap molasses
I ¼ cup skim milk
I cup self-rising flour

put the bran flakes, sugar, figs, molasses, and skim milk into a bowl. Mix well together and leave to stand for half an hour. Sift in the flour, mixing it well.

put the mixture into a greased 1 pound loaf pan and bake in a preheated moderate oven at 350°F for 45–60 minutes.

turn out of the pan and allow to cool. Serve sliced, and spread with low-fat spread, if desired.

Makes 1 x 1 pound loaf (8 slices per loaf)
Preparation time: *20 minutes, plus standing*
Cooking time: *45–60 minutes*
Oven temperature: *350°F*

per slice: *protein 5 g • fat 1 g • cholest. 39 g*

Date Loaf

1 cup chopped dates
¾ cup cold tea
2 cups whole-wheat flour
4 teaspoons baking powder
1 teaspoon ground mixed spice
¾ cup soft brown sugar
1 egg, lightly beaten
1 tablespoon soft brown sugar

put the dates in a bowl, pour the tea over them, and leave to soak for 2 hours. Add the remaining ingredients, except the soft brown sugar, and mix thoroughly.

turn into a lined and greased 2-pound loaf pan. Sprinkle with the soft brown sugar and bake in a preheated oven at 350°F for 1–1¼ hours.

leave in the pan for 5 minutes, then turn on to a wire rack to cool.

serve sliced and spread with low-fat spread, if liked.

Makes 1 x 2-pound loaf (15 slices per loaf)
Preparation time: *10 minutes, plus soaking*
Cooking time: *1–1¼ hours*
Oven temperature: *350°F*

per slice: *protein 6 g • fat 2 g • cholest. 67 g*

Whole-wheat Bread

12 cups whole-wheat flour
2 teaspoons salt
2 packages dry yeast
1 teaspoon brown sugar or dark molasses
1 quart warm water
beaten egg, to glaze
a little buckwheat, for sprinkling (optional)

mix together the flour, salt, and yeast in a large warmed bowl. Add the brown sugar or molasses to the measured water in a bowl, and stir into the flour to make a soft pliable dough.

knead the dough on a lightly floured surface for 10 minutes until smooth and elastic. Return to the clean bowl and cover with lightly oiled plastic wrap, or a plastic bag. Leave in a warm place for 1 hour, or until the dough has doubled in bulk.

turn the dough on to a lightly floured surface and cut in half. Knead each piece until smooth, then place in two 2-pound loaf pans. Place the pans in a large, lightly oiled plastic bag and tie loosely. Leave in a warm place until the dough rises above the sides of the pan.

brush the loaves with beaten egg and sprinkle with buckwheat, if using. Bake in a preheated oven at 425°F for 30–45 minutes. Leave to cool on a wire rack.

Makes 2 x 2-pound loaves (15 slices per loaf)
Preparation time: *30 minutes, plus proving*
Cooking time: *30–45 minutes*
Oven temperature: *425°F*

per slice: *protein 6.4 g • fat 1 g • cholest. 34 g*

Broths and Dressings

Chicken Broth

1 whole chicken carcass

3½ quarts water

1 teaspoon salt

1 Bermuda onion, peeled and stuck with 4 cloves

2 celery sticks, chopped

2 carrots, coarsely chopped

2 sprigs of parsley

1 bouquet garni

1 bayleaf

8 black peppercorns

put the carcass into a deep saucepan, cover with the water, and add the salt. Bring to a boil, skimming off the scum with a slotted spoon. Reduce the heat, partially cover the pan, and simmer for 1 hour.

add the onion, celery, carrots, parsley, bouquet garni, bayleaf, and peppercorns. Stir and continue simmering, partially covered, for a further 1½-2 hours. Add more water if the level drops below the bones.

cool slightly. Remove the carcass, then strain the broth through a fine sieve into a bowl, discarding all the vegetables and herbs. After straining the broth, pick over the carcass, remove any meat still on the bones, and add it to the broth.

leave to cool, then skim off the fat with a spoon or blot with paper towels. Cover the broth, refrigerate it, and use within 3 days. This broth is suitable for freezing — if frozen use within 3 months.

Makes about *3½ quarts*
Preparation time: *5–8 minutes*
Cooking time: *about 2½–3 hours*

(with fat removed) • *protein 12 g* • *fat 5 g* • *cholest. 2 g*

Vegetable Broth

3 medium potatoes, chopped

1 medium onion, finely sliced

2 leeks, chopped

2 celery sticks, chopped

2 medium carrots, chopped

1 small head of fennel, finely sliced

thyme, parsley stalks, and 2 bayleaves

1½ quarts water

salt and pepper

put all the vegetables into a pan with the herbs and the water. Bring to a boil slowly, then skim. Add salt and pepper to taste. Simmer for about 1½ hours, covered,

skimming the broth three or four times during cooking.

strain the broth through clean cheesecloth or a very fine sieve. Cool and store in the refrigerator until required.

Makes about 1 quart
Preparation time: *10 minutes*
Cooking time: *1½ hours*

protein 2 g • fat 3 g • cholest. 2 g

Fish Broth

2 pounds fish trimmings
I small onion, peeled and minced
2 leeks, chopped
I bayleaf
parsley stalks, sprigs of fennel and lemon rind
1½ quarts water
I cup dry white wine
salt and pepper

place the fish trimmings in a large saucepan with the onion, leeks, bayleaf, parsley stalks, sprigs of fennel, lemon rind, and water. Bring to a boil slowly, then skim any surface scum.

add the white wine, and salt and pepper to taste and simmer very gently for 30 minutes, skimming the broth once or twice during cooking. Strain the broth through clean cheesecloth or a very fine sieve. Cool and keep chilled until needed.

Makes about 1 quart
Preparation time: *15 minutes*
Cooking time: *45 minutes*

protein 0 g • fat 0 g • cholest. 0 g

Tomato Sauce

1 medium onion, chopped

2 tablespoons olive oil

1 garlic clove, crushed (optional)

3 cups tomatoes, skinned and seeded

1 tablespoon chopped fresh basil

⅔ cup red wine or Chicken Broth (see page 244)

½ teaspoon soft dark brown sugar

1 tablespoon tomato paste

½ teaspoon grated orange rind

salt and freshly ground black pepper

fry the onion gently in the oil for 3 minutes. Add the garlic, if desired, and the tomatoes and basil, and cook together for a further 2 minutes.

add the remaining ingredients and simmer gently for 25 minutes, until the sauce is soft and pulpy.

press the sauce through a sieve.

reheat the sauce if a hot sauce is required; otherwise cover it and store in a refrigerator.

Makes approximately 1¾ cups
Preparation time: *10 minutes*
Cooking time: *30 minutes*

each of 6 portions: • *protein 1 g* • *fat 4 g* • *cholest. 6 g*

clipboard: This sauce is much easier to sieve if it is first blended in a blender or food processor.

Low-Calorie French Dressing

2 tablespoons olive oil

6 tablespoons wine vinegar

½ teaspoon mustard

¼ teaspoon sugar

salt and freshly ground black pepper

place all the ingredients, with salt and pepper to taste, in a screw-top jar and shake vigorously until well blended.

Makes ½ cup
Preparation time: *5 minutes*

per dessert spoon: • *protein 0 g* • *fat 1 g* • *cholest. 0 g*

Homemade Yogurt

2½ cups semi-skim milk
1½ tablespoons plain low-fat live yogurt

put the milk into a pan and bring just to a boil; allow to cool to body temperature.

lightly whisk in the live yogurt until thoroughly mixed.

pour into a wide-necked vacuum flask, and seal securely.

leave to stand undisturbed for about 10 hours or overnight.

keep the yogurt in the refrigerator for up to 4 days.

Makes about 2½ cups
Preparation time: *10 minutes, plus fermenting*
Cooking time: *1 minute*

each of 6 portions:• *protein 4 g • fat 2 g • cholest. 6 g*

clipboard: Yogurt is a fermented milk product. The fermenting agent is a little fresh yogurt, which is added to the milk. You can, of course, use your own homemade yogurt as the fermenting agent for making more.

Tomato Juice Dressing

½ cup tomato juice

½ cup wine vinegar

1 teaspoon grated onion

½ teaspoon dried mustard

½ teaspoon sugar

½ teaspoon Worcestershire sauce

1 teaspoon minced fresh parsley

salt and pepper

beat the tomato juice with the vinegar, grated onion, mustard, sugar, Worcestershire sauce, parsley, and salt and pepper, to taste, until well blended. Alternatively, place all the ingredients in a screw-top jar and shake vigorously to combine well before using.

Makes 1 cup
preparation time: *10 minutes*

kcal 54 • KJ 228 • protein 2 g • fat 1 g
  • cholest. 10 g

Lemon and Yogurt Dressing

⅔ cup plain low-fat yogurt
1 tablespoon lemon juice
2 tablespoons chopped mixed fresh herbs
salt and black pepper

combine all the ingredients in a bowl, whisking well with a fork.

cover with plastic wrap and chill in the refrigerator until ready to serve.

Makes 1 cup
Preparation time: *5 minutes, plus chilling*

protein 89 g • fat 1 g • cholest. 12 g

clipboard: There are many possible variations on this dressing. Use mint instead of mixed herbs for cucumber salads, basil for tomato salads, and parsley for green salads or potato salads.

Low-Calorie Vinaigrette

2 tablespoons lemon juice
3 tablespoons olive oil
1 teaspoon Dijon-style mustard
1 garlic clove, crushed
1 tablespoon minced parsley (optional)
1 tablespoon minced chives (optional)
salt and freshly ground black pepper

beat the lemon juice with the olive oil, mustard, garlic, chopped herbs, if using, and salt and pepper to taste, until well blended. Alternatively, place all the ingredients in a screw-top jar and shake vigorously to combine well before using.

Makes ⅓ cup
Preparation time: *5 minutes*

per dessertspoon:• *protein 3 g • fat 3 g • cholest. 0 g*

Low-calorie Blender Mayonnaise

1 egg
salt and pepper
½ teaspoon dried mustard
4 tablespoons olive oil
2 tablespoons lemon juice

place the egg, salt, pepper, and mustard in a blender. Process for a few seconds. Remove the center cap from the lid and gradually add the oil with the motor still running on low speed.

gradually add the lemon juice until the mixture is thick. Serve at once or keep for up to 1 week in a screw-top jar in the refrigerator.

Makes ½ cup

per tablespoon:• *protein 0 g • fat 5 g • cholest. 0 g*

clipboard: Ring the changes according to what you are serving this with. For a curry mayonnaise, for example, replace the mustard power with curry powder to taste. For a herb mayonnaise, add ½ tablespoon of very finely chopped fresh herbs after the lemon juice.

Index